*Deacons in the Liturgy*

# DEACONS
# IN THE LITURGY

*second edition*

ORMONDE PLATER

Church Publishing
NEW YORK

Unless otherwise noted, the Scripture quotations contained herein are from the *New Revised Standard Version* Bible, copyright © 1989 by the Division of Christian Education of the National Council of Churches of Christ in the U.S.A. Used by permission. All rights reserved.

Library of Congress Cataloging-in-Publication Data
Plater, Ormonde.
Deacons in the liturgy / Ormonde Plater. — 2nd ed.
    p.    cm.
ISBN 978-0-89869-634-9 (pbk.)
1. Deacons—Episcopal Church. 2. Deacons—Anglican Church of Canada. 3. Deacons—Anglican Communion. 4. Episcopal Church —Liturgy. 5. Anglican Church of Canada—Liturgy. 6. Anglican Communion—Liturgy. I. Title.
BX5967.5.P53 2009
264'.03—dc22
                                                2009005857

*Printed in the United States of America.*

Cover design by Christina Hope
Interior design by Vicki K. Black

Church Publishing, Incorporated
445 Fifth Avenue
New York, New York 10016
www.churchpublishing.com

5  4  3  2  1

# CONTENTS

# FOREWORD

DURING THE MANY years I was actively waiting for the diaconate to become a reality in my diocese, I was given a pearl of wisdom from a presbyter who quietly offered support for nearly a decade before that reality would come to be. On one occasion when I thanked him for that support, he wrote, "The church has sometimes done a very good job of reaching down—but not out." It was with that pearl nestled nearby that I would come to understand the words in the ordination service for a deacon, and especially the charges in the examination: "You are to assist the bishop and priests in public worship and in the ministration of God's Word and Sacraments."

In our culture, jobs in the "service sector" and realities such as "public assistance" carry with them implicit distinctions in class, that is, in power and economy. Often those distinctions travel right into our church. They influence, sometimes deeply, the way we interpret the word "servanthood," or even the word "assist." The pearl that I carried with me enabled me to see that the deacon's role in liturgy is not so much about helping, but about "attending." Not so much about assisting those higher in rank, but about coming alongside (*parakaleo* in the

Greek) in a way that allows us to be seen in the periphery—
not down below, but at the side, prepared to make sure the
celebration of the whole Body is done thoughtfully, faithfully,
with attention to detail. Not with fussiness, but with grace.

In this revised version of his *Deacons in the Liturgy*, Ormonde Plater continues to capture the depth and richness in
the liturgy where all the roles, of every order, are afforded their
distinctive places. While the title of the book points primarily
to the place of deacons in the liturgy, it is so much more. It is
a book that points toward the liturgy through a diaconal lens,
and embraces the fullness of all that the 1979 *Book of Common Prayer* has brought us by restoring (as Plater wrote in his
introduction to the last edition) "the diversity of ministries as
a cardinal principle of worship."

As a beneficiary of Ormonde's teaching and writing, his de-
votion to the diaconate in all its fullness, and his scholarship,
as well as a friend and colleague, I commend this new revision
to you. I suspect that as you read and reread this little book
you will find that, in addition to learning the importance of actions and assignments in the liturgy, the very richness of the orders themselves will seep into your understanding of corporate
worship.

—*Susanne Watson Epting*

# PREFACE

FOR MANY YEARS I have heard two complaints about deacons. Bishops and priests complain that deacons don't know how to do their job in liturgy. Deacons complain that bishops and priests won't let them do their job in liturgy.

The solution lies not in grumbling or in unhealthy restrictions and substitutions, but in liturgical formation, both theological and practical, for bishops, priests, deacons, and indeed for all the people of God. This book is designed to help provide such formation.

The need for formation appeared early in the modern revival of the diaconate. In 1980 the National Center for the Diaconate (since 1985 the North American Association for the Diaconate) asked me to write a liturgical manual for use in the Episcopal Church, published the following year as *The Deacon in the Liturgy*. A decade later I completely revised the manual as a small book called *Deacons in the Liturgy* (Morehouse Publishing, 1992). Now, sixteen years later, I have visited this subject yet again for a major revision.

The reasons are several. Among them has been my experience as an archdeacon during 1998–2005. Acting as deputy for my bishop, Charles Jenkins of Louisiana, I prepared for and took part in convention liturgies, ordinations, and other large services. Accompanying my bishop on visits to congregations, I learned that each place, small or large, eccentric or stodgy, has its own way of doing everything in a rich gumbo of local customs. Although worship stands on the firm ground of ancient tradition, it always takes place in a particular time and place in which particular peoples live. It must respect and draw upon the local culture, adapting old ways to the native way of life. I am grateful to the parishes of St. Anna's, Grace, and Trinity in New Orleans, where, over thirty-seven years, I discovered what diversity of culture means and found freedom to learn the liturgical role of deacon as it needed to be performed in those places. There are few practices in this book that I have not used in the regular worship of real congregations.

Among deacons at large, a new generation has come along. Deeply engaged in ministry in the world, leading people in that ministry, they appreciate the connections between bread for the poor and bread for the faithful. To bring life and clarity to these connections in the Christian assembly, they need to do their role in liturgy better. There have also been changes and additions to official liturgies of the Episcopal Church and other Anglican churches, with new editions of supplemental books.

In several ways, therefore, this recension of *Deacons in the Liturgy* is a new book, expressing the ideal of liturgy as it might be celebrated in God's new world, adjusted to the flickering shadows of liturgy as it actually is celebrated, a book extensively revised, rephrased, and expanded. I have added an appendix containing summaries of the deacon's functions in the Eucharist, baptism, Holy Week liturgies, visitations of the bishop, and ordinations, and cartoons showing when bishops have their "Hats Off!" and "Sticks On!" (created by Priscilla Maumus, a deacon of the diocese of Louisiana).

Two persons read the manuscript for errors and suggestions. The Reverend Leonel L. Mitchell, Professor Emeritus of Liturgics at Seabury-Western Theological Seminary, brought his deep and practical knowledge of the liturgical traditions of the church. Deacon Susanne Watson Epting, Executive Director of the North American Association for the Diaconate, contributed the perspective of an experienced and authoritative deacon. This book is designed for use both in the Episcopal Church and in the Anglican Church of Canada. Page references point to the principal liturgical books in those two churches.

—*Ormonde Plater*
*The Feast of St. Francis of Assisi 2008*

# INTRODUCTION

AMONG MANY REFORMS of a catholic nature, the *Book of Common Prayer* adopted by the Episcopal Church in 1979 restored diversity of ministries as a cardinal principle of worship. There had been a long interval without this virtue. Replacing the Latin Mass in England, the 1549 prayer book assumed as the norm a solemn and corporate form of the Eucharist, with priests, deacons, and clerks (singers) taking their customary roles. In 1552 and thereafter, in the Church of England and eventually in her daughters and sisters of the Anglican Communion, bishops, priests or presbyters, deacons, and other baptized persons performed liturgical roles (when they had them) inconsistent with a serious theology of the body of Christ. Prayer books in England and elsewhere provided a eucharistic liturgy closely related to the medieval Low Mass, in which the people, even when present, hardly mattered except as passive recipients of sacramental grace. In the official Anglican Eucharist, for four centuries, the priest recited most of the liturgy solo while the people listened or read along. Unofficially, at least after the Oxford Movement in the nineteenth century, liturgy was often crowded with people and lively in ceremony.

The enhanced use of deacons is a notable aspect of re-formed liturgy. In the 1549 prayer book, deacons (vested in the old "Albes with tunacles") performed traditional functions. Afterward, deacons virtually disappeared. In a period extending from the English prayer book of 1662 through the American prayer book of 1928, deacons assisted in the Eucharist, but the only functions clearly assigned them were to receive the alms, bring them to the priest, and help in the distribution of communion. In the twentieth century, liturgical renewal led in a few places to official recovery of diaconal functions—usually reading the gospel, sometimes saying intercessory prayers or leading the general confession. These deacons functioned mainly as assistant ministers of the word. Meanwhile, Anglo-Catholic missals and manuals such as E. C. R. Lamburn's *Ritual Notes* (1894) and Percy Dearmer's *Parson's Handbook* (1899), both reissued in several editions, showed the way toward recovery of solemn celebrations with medieval Roman and Sarum ceremonies, although the liturgical deacons were usually priests in diaconal vestments.

Then came the Second Vatican Council in 1962–1965 and the restoration of the permanent diaconate in the Roman Catholic Church in 1967. About the same time, the Episcopal Church began to experience a revival of diverse ministries and to experiment with rites that made full use of deacons and other ministers. Carefully revised, these rites formed the heart of the *Book of Common Prayer* authorized in 1979.

Other volumes provide additions or alternatives to the prayer book liturgies. *The Book of Occasional Services 2003* (BOS) is an official supplement containing seasonal, pastoral, and episcopal liturgies (Church Publishing, 2004). Because

General Convention authorizes additional material, usually every three years, this volume is frequently revised. A new revision, being prepared for presentation to General Convention in 2009, was not available during the writing of this guide for deacons. Several books under the general title *Enriching Our Worship,* authorized by General Convention, contain material for "worshiping communities wishing to expand the language, images and metaphors used in worship" (EOW1 5).

The liturgies of the Anglican Church of Canada use deacons in ways similar to those of the Episcopal Church. The Canadian church published *The Book of Alternative Services* (BAS) in 1985, widely used as a replacement for their 1962 prayer book, and a supplemental volume, *Occasional Celebrations,* in 1992, followed by several booklets of supplemental liturgies.

*Deacons in the Liturgy* is a guide for use alongside the canonical books of liturgy. Deacons, presiders, and other planners of liturgy may use this book along with other guides: Howard E. Galley,[1] *The Ceremonies of the Eucharist: A Guide to Celebration* (Cowley Publications, 1989); Leonel L. Mitchell, *Lent, Holy Week, Easter, and the Great Fifty Days* (Cowley Publications, 1996); Leonel L. Mitchell, *Pastoral and Occasional Liturgies* (Cowley Publications, 1998); Paul V. Marshall, *The Bishop Is Coming!* (Church Publishing, 2007); and Patrick Malloy, *Celebrating the Eucharist: A Practical Ceremonial Guide for Clergy and Other Liturgical Ministers* (Church Publishing, 2007). Also helpful is the principal manual in the Church of England, *Celebrating the Eucharist* by Benjamin Gordon-Taylor and Simon Jones, Alcuin Liturgy Guides 3 (SPCK, 2005). Howard E. Galley's *The Prayer Book Office* (Seabury, 1980) contains many enrichments of the daily office but is out of print. For bishops, their deacons, and others who work with bishops, I recommend the Roman Catholic *Ceremonial of Bishops* (The Liturgical Press, 1989); allowing for Anglican differences in some rites, it fills in a lot of gaps. Above all, I urge deacons and all others who love liturgy to keep at their bedside and taste frequently Aidan Kavanagh's wise and witty guide, *Elements of Rite* (Pueblo, 1982).

Three major characteristics motivate the way deacons are used in liturgy. First, deacons are many in the life of the church. Where once we could speak of the *deacon* in the liturgy, as if most congregations had only one (if they had any), now we must sometimes speak of *deacons.* The plural refers to a modest number, appropriate to the dignity and restrained style of Anglican liturgy. A generation ago it was rare to see a deacon in a congregation; now it is common to see two or more. Dioceses have official communities of deacons, a natural gathering now recognized by canon law. Plurality of service also has precedent in scripture. Jesus sent disciples out by twos to bring the good news and to prepare the Passover meal. In serving by twos or more, and not just in liturgies with a bishop, deacons symbolize the number and diversity of all Christian ministries of word, care, and worship.

Second, deacons serve with priests, deacons, and other baptized persons. In liturgy, deacons always perform in relationship with others. They work with others to adapt, compose, and lead the prayers of intercession. With others they wait on table, so that the entire assembly can offer a sacrifice of praise and thanksgiving. Joining with others, they serve the messianic meal and send waiters out of the assembly to feed absent brothers and sisters with the body and blood of Christ. By working together in liturgy, deacons and others symbolize the mission of the church in the world.

Third, deacons tend to be vigorous, plain, and practical. That's their style as they serve the bishop, the church, and the poor, and that's their distinctive style as they serve the assembly in word and sacrament.

This book thus has several purposes: to help deacons serve in the liturgy with grace and manners, sensitive to the needs of the presider and the people; to help communities of faith use their deacons in ways appropriate to the dignity and meaning of the order; to help communities without the diaconate discover how deacons enhance the liturgy; and to help all Christians—bishops, priests, deacons, and all the baptized—express baptismal ministry in the life and worship of the church.

Deacons are members of a sacred order dating from the first century. Although their liturgical role continues to evolve in small and careful ways, the essential shape of the role has remained intact since the early church. This book honors the great tradition that has come down to us through the *Book of Common Prayer* of the Episcopal Church and the *Book of Alternative Services* of the Anglican Church of Canada. Wherever that tradition allows, and the occasion is appropriate, I have adapted material from the current *Missale Romanum,* the Ambrosian rite of Northern Italy, the Mozarabic rite of old Spain, the Orthodox liturgy, and a few other ancient sources.

My own preferences are transparent. They are catholic and traditional but not afraid of change. My motto: When in doubt, do it!

1

# GENERAL NORMS

## ORDINARY FUNCTIONS

Deacons are the principal assistants, the most active of all who serve in the liturgy. They are heralds of the word, servants of the church, and agents of the bishop. Deacons act for the good of others by setting them free for worship of God and action in the world. At the ordination of deacons, the bishop tells the ordinands: "You are to assist the bishop and priests in public worship and in the ministration of God's Word and Sacraments" (BCP 543; BAS 655). The presence of deacons, however, goes beyond mere assistance. It imparts a special quality that rises to the level of symbol.

As symbols, deacons embody two ancient concepts, angels and waiters. They are messengers and heralds of the word. They proclaim the good news of God in Christ and interpret the world to the community of faith. They oversee the sacrificial meal, wait on table, prepare, serve, and clean up. They enable the hungry to eat and the thirsty to drink, as they serve in the sacramental liturgies of the church and among God's poor in the world. Both angel and waiter appear in every deacon in every diaconal role and function in every liturgy.

Deacons' roles in liturgy reflect their roles outside the liturgy. The bishop presides in all liturgies because the bishop presides in the diocese, and the priest presides in the Eucharist and other congregational liturgies because the priest presides in the congregation. Deacons serve in liturgy because deacons mobilize the church, especially for works of love in the world.

Works of love for those in need, with emphasis on "the poor, the sick, the suffering, and the helpless" (BCP 510; BAS 631), focus in worship through the liturgical words and actions of deacons. In this way the messiness of human existence, filled with complexity, ambiguity, and contradiction, enters Christian liturgy, and Christian people present God's creation to God for the salvation of God's people. In this way, too, deacons reveal the *diakonia* of Christ as God's agent in creation and salvation, God's face reflected in the faces of God's people. The role of deacons in the liturgy reveals the nature of deacons as proclaimers and evangelists, messengers and bearers of the good news to the poor, and servants in the image of Christ.

Deacons serve in an assembly of faithful worshipers. With kindness and respect they submit to the customs of the congregation and the practices of the priest in charge. Never competing with others for place and prerogative in liturgy, they enlist and involve other baptized persons in proper liturgical roles, as in ministries of mercy and justice.

The liturgical role of deacons comes to us partly by descent from the early church, especially of the first four centuries, and partly by intelligent reform in our own age. The text and rubrics of each rite, especially the Eucharist and the Ordination of Deacons, clearly reveal the essential or ordinary functions of deacons. These occur in two main groups, Liturgy of the Word and Liturgy of the Sacrament.

## LITURGY OF THE WORD
Deacons proclaim the word of God, assuming the role of angel, messenger, and bearer of good news. Specifically they act as:

### (1) Reader of the gospel
A deacon normally proclaims the gospel reading. There are three main exceptions:

   (a) In the absence of a deacon functioning liturgically, the presider or an assisting priest reads the gospel.

   (b) Other baptized persons may read or sing the passion gospel on Palm Sunday and Good Friday.

   (c) When part of a congregation speaks a foreign language, another person may read the gospel in that tongue (perhaps in addition to the gospel in English).

### (2) Occasional preacher
Preaching is normally a function of the presider. Bishops and priests preach because they are ordained for that task, without excluding others from the function. The bishop may license other baptized persons to preach, and in some places gifted persons preach at the invitation of the presider. Deacons preach as gifted persons, as agents of the bishop, or as those

whose duty is "to make Christ and his redemptive love known" (BCP 543; BAS 655). In some dioceses, the bishop assumes that deacons have the right to preach by the authority of their ordination; in others, the bishop licenses or otherwise grants deacons the faculty of preaching.

### (3) Leader of intercessions
A deacon is the ordinary leader of the biddings inviting the people to pray for those in need. Other baptized persons may also lead the prayers of the people, or a deacon and others may share in leading the prayers.

### (4) Herald
Deacons announce, exhort, call to worship, invite confession, instruct, keep order, and act as master of ceremonies. (Some places with large or at least formal celebrations use another person to act as master of ceremonies.) By overseeing many practical details of worship, deacons enable priests and bishops to preside prayerfully and help the people to take part actively. It is an old custom for deacons to announce the feasts of the church year, and on the holiest of nights, at the Great Vigil of Easter, they proclaim the paschal feast by chanting the Exsultet.

### LITURGY OF THE SACRAMENT
Deacons serve the table, assuming the role of butler of the house, *maître d'hôtel,* and steward of the banquet. Specifically they act as:

*(1) Headwaiter*
Deacons prepare the table, receive, prepare, and place on it the bread and wine. After the meal they eat and drink the remaining bread and wine (aside from what is to be kept) and cleanse the vessels. Typically, others help with these functions.

*(2) Steward of the wine*
Standing at the presider's right, a deacon raises the cup during the doxology (ending words of praise) of the eucharistic prayer and at the invitation to communion. At communion, deacons normally give the wine to the faithful, and they may also give the bread. At a large celebration, with several deacons and priests, some may serve the bread and some the wine. Other persons licensed by the bishop (called eucharistic ministers) may give the wine "in the absence of sufficient deacons and priests" (BCP 408); canon law permits them also to give the bread. The Canadian church allows persons authorized by the bishop to give communion (BAS 183).

*(3) Dismisser*
A deacon ends the liturgy by telling the people to go or inviting them to "bless the Lord." The dismissal is part of a deacon's angelic role of making announcements, exhorting, giving directions to come and go and to use certain gestures and postures, and otherwise aiding the active participation of the people.

*(4) Minister of the reserved sacrament*
After their ordination, new deacons have the privilege of carrying the reserved sacrament "to those communicants who, be-

cause of sickness or other grave cause, could not be present" (BCP 555). The Canadian church omits the provision. This continues to be a function of deacons during their lifetime of ordained ministry. Deacons also oversee the work of eucharistic visitors, those licensed to bring the sacrament to the absent. Many congregations reserve the sacrament in a tabernacle or aumbry. For easy access during the week, deacons may reserve it at home in a safe place, marked by a lamp or icon. The older custom was to keep the sacrament only under the form of bread, easy to carry and give, but increasingly the consecrated wine is also reserved. Deacons and other ministers carry the bread in a small metal or ceramic box called a pyx (Latin *pyxis* or box). They may carry the wine in a small bottle, or intinct (dip) pieces of bread in the wine before taking it to communicants.

## DEACONS AND THE BISHOP

Deacons act as emissaries and deputies of the bishop, and this relationship is reflected in their liturgical role. From Ignatius of Antioch at the beginning of the second century, deacons have stood in a special place alongside the bishop, representing closeness and solidarity in ministry. At their ordination, the bishop tells the ordinands: "God now calls you to a special ministry of servanthood [*diakonia*] directly under your bishop" (BCP 543, see BAS 655), a phrase stressing line of authority. Two deacons normally attend the bishop as presider of any liturgy, while in the Eucharist another serves as liturgical deacon. Even if priests are present, deacons serve in their proper role and functions. Deacons especially help the bishop at ordinations. In the rites for investing and seating a diocesan bishop, the number of attendants is set at two deacons (BOS 349, 357).

## WORSHIP SPACE

Most worship spaces are arranged in one of three ways, emphasizing different locations and orientations (both spatial and theological) for offering prayer:

*(1) Versus populum (toward the people)*
Presider and deacon face the people across a freestanding altar, emphasizing the presence of Christ in the gathered assembly. In most places, during the Liturgy of the Word the presider and deacon occupy chairs facing the people.

*(2) Ad orientem (toward the actual or liturgical east)*
Presider and deacon, at the head of all the people, face the east end of the space (where the altar is located against the wall or freestanding), place of the rising sun and risen Christ. In most places, during the Liturgy of the Word the presider and deacon occupy chairs on the side of the altar space, facing inward or toward the people.

*(3) In medio populi (in the middle of the people)*
The people, including presider and deacon, face a central space, either in two lines (antiphonal, as in monastic worship) or in the round, or as a combination of both. Everyone, in-

cluding presider and deacon, faces the center of the church, toward the real presence of Christ in word and on the altar. During the Liturgy of the Word the presider and deacon occupy chairs on one side or at one end or within the circle.

## MOVEMENT AND GESTURES

Deacons normally sit to hear the word read and preached. They stand to perform duties and to pray, even during the eucharistic prayer.[2] In practice many Roman Catholic deacons remain standing. Anglican deacons preferably stand throughout the prayer to emphasize its unity.

In a procession, the deacon carrying the gospel book walks just ahead of the presider, other deacons, and concelebrating bishops and priests. If not carrying the gospel book, the deacon walks beside the presider. If the presider is a bishop, two attending deacons walk a little behind the bishop. In a procession with the paschal candle, the deacon bears the lighted candle and leads the procession (in place of the cross), perhaps behind a thurifer.

A single deacon usually sits at the presider's right, and two deacons sit on either side. During the Liturgy of the Word, however, deacons may remain closer to the people, as in the Orthodox liturgy. Deacons' seats should be visible and preferably face the people. Like other ministerial leaders, deacons sit upright and place their hands on their knees (which are never crossed).

During the Liturgy of the Sacrament, deacons stand and move near the altar. At the altar the normal position of the deacon assisting with the cup is at the presider's right, two or three steps back. A deacon assisting with the book stands on the left in the same position. They step forward to handle the cup and turn pages. (With the Altar Book placed on the left, a single deacon may walk to that side as needed to turn pages, unless someone else turns them.) Since in many churches the freestanding altar is near the back wall, deacons may have to stand two or three steps to the side rather than to the back. In churches celebrating *ad orientem,* deacons stand a step to the side and one step down (or back), facing east. When addressing the people, deacons turn to face the people.

While standing, except when performing a function requiring hands, deacons hold hands joined, fingers interlocking or palm to palm, following the presider's preference.[3] In the early church, in most places, during prayer all persons stood facing east (hence, they were *oriented*) and held their hands raised and extended to the side, palms turned forward and upward. When leading the prayers of the people, standing in the midst of the people and facing east, a deacon may use this *orans* or prayer gesture.

As much as possible, deacons should be familiar with the words, music, and rubrics of the liturgy. They should memorize their parts and listen attentively while others read scripture or lead song or prayer. It is distracting for liturgical leaders to carry or gaze at books and leaflets, including the *Book of Common Prayer* or *Book of Alternative Services,* unless those publications are needed for a particular function.

Decisions about movement depend on the reality of the worship space as well as on ancient tradition. What is the size and configuration of this space? What is its lighting and capacity for sound? How should the presider and deacon, and others, stand and move? How do people see the action and participate in the liturgy?

## VESTMENTS

The historic vestments of deacons in the western church are the alb and the dalmatic. In a practice originating in the eastern church and now universally observed, deacons also wear a stole over the left shoulder.

Deacons wear vestments in all liturgies. At their ordination the ordinands wear as their base garment a surplice over a cassock or (more commonly) an alb. After the prayer of consecration, the new deacons receive a "stole worn over the left shoulder, or other insignia of the office of deacon" (BCP 536, 554; see BAS 666). This confusing rubric reflects a long and complicated historical development and a diversity of styles, including alb, dalmatic, and stole in the West and *sticharion* and *orarion* in the East.

The alb (Latin *albus,* white) signifies the white robe originally given to each new Christian at baptism. Worn as an undergarment (the medieval way), the alb is simple, lightweight, and girded with a white rope; it may include a hood or neckband or a separate neckpiece, the amice (Latin *amictus* or mantle). Worn as an outer garment (a modern development of the ancient style), the alb is heavier, attractive in fabric and cut, and often ungirded; it may reach the appearance and dimension of a dalmatic with a collar or hood and wide sleeves. In the frigid buildings of northern Europe, wearing heavy garments under the alb eventually turned that ancient dress into a surplice (Latin *superpellicium* or overcoat), now usually worn over a cassock.

The "other insignia" include the dalmatic (originally a tunic of white wool from the province of Dalmatia on the eastern coast of the Adriatic Sea), the outer garment of deacons in the western church. Instead of alb and dalmatic, eastern deacons wear the *sticharion,* a colorful, textured tunic often depicted in icons. Like all other vestments, the dalmatic changed over the centuries until it became heavy, highly ornamented, and short in both length and sleeves. When western deacons adopted the stole, sometime after the sixth century, for several centuries they wore it on top of the dalmatic. By the late Middle Ages deacons were wearing an ornate dalmatic in the color of the day, open at the sides, with the stole underneath.

In many places today, the medieval style has given way to the primitive dalmatic. This garment is an ample white or off-white tunic, simple, sober, and functional, often with the stole on top. The early dalmatic included wide sleeves with bands about the cuffs and *clavi,* or colored stripes, descending from the shoulders to the hem. The sixth-century mosaic of bishop Maximianus and his two deacons at San Vitale in Ravenna shows all three in dalmatics of this style. Modern dalmatics often omit the bands and stripes. The result is sometimes a single garment, a dalmatic-like tunic called by clerical outfitters a "contemporary alb" or "sanctuary alb." In their design and manufacture, dalmatics and other vestments ought to reflect local culture as well as ancient tradition. When handmade of natural fabrics, vestments show our concern for the beauty and preservation of God's creation.

Deacons may wear a dalmatic at all celebrations of the Eucharist and on other solemn occasions, including Evensong. A good rule of thumb is: When the presider wears a chasuble or cope, the deacon may wear a dalmatic. In practice, the dalmatic is often reserved for occasions of great solemnity.

At celebrations of the daily office, Anglican tradition since the Reformation calls for wearing a cassock, surplice, tippet, and academic hood. Roman Catholic and Lutheran clergy usually wear an alb and stole of the day. Increasingly, especially at ecumenical gatherings, alb and stole are acceptable for Anglicans.

The stole (Latin *stola* or garment) is an insignia of office. It may have begun in the East as an ornate toga, folded and drawn about the body, which developed into a ceremonial scarf. In the eastern church the deacon's stole is called *orarion* (Latin *orare,* to speak or to pray), signifying the deacon's role in the gospel and litanies. Like the wings of a seraph, the eastern deacon wraps *orarion* over *sticharion.* When the deacon moves about the stole flutters, and when chanting a litany the deacon holds one end in three fingers of the right hand, like a folded wing.

Deacons wear the stole over the left shoulder in one of three ways:

*(1) Ends tied or attached under the right arm*
In the late classical age, western deacons added the eastern stole to the Roman dalmatic, wearing it on top. A tenth-century illumination at the Vatican library shows the deacon at the Easter Vigil wearing his stole over his dalmatic, hanging straight down from the left shoulder.[4] Later, when deacons wore the stole under the dalmatic,

they tied the ends under the right arm to keep them out
of the way.

*(2) Straight down from the left shoulder*
As in the illustration mentioned above, this was the
original way that Roman deacons wore their stole.
Ordinary deacons in Russia and some other places in the
East (except Greece) still wear the *orarion* hanging
straight. This stole is usually four to five inches wide and
about ten feet long, made of brocade with seven crosses
embroidered or appliquéd along its length. Occasionally
the word "Holy" will be embroidered three times on it in
large letters. To stay put, the fabric needs to be heavy or
rough, or deacons may use a patch of velcro on the
shoulder.

*(3) Wrapped around the body*
In the so-called Byzantine style deacons wear a long stole
with the middle under the right arm and the ends
hanging front and back from the left shoulder. This stole
is the double *orarion,* originally two stoles sewed end to
end. Russian archdeacons and protodeacons wear it as a
mark of dignity. The style spread to the Greek church,
and in Greek practice all deacons wear the double
*orarion.* Many deacons in the Episcopal Church wear the
double *orarion,* and it is also worn by permanent deacons
serving at the Cathedral of Notre Dame in Paris.[5]

Crosses and similar religious ornaments are personal adorn-
ments, worn only beneath vestments. Before the liturgy deacons ought to remove their wristwatches, bracelets, dangling
earrings, and other distracting jewelry. Except in some Anglo-

Catholic congregations, maniples are an anachronism no longer worn.

The deacon's stole often obstructs the right side of the body. It is better to wear electronic controls—such as the switch for a small microphone—on the left side, where the deacon can reach them easily beneath vestments.

In the absence of a deacon, assisting priests who perform diaconal functions vest as priests, to avoid being mistaken for deacons. It is also confusing for anyone to vest as subdeacon, a minor order abolished in the Church of England in 1550 and in the Latin Rite of the Catholic Church in 1972; an exception may be made for Anglo-Catholic masses using three sacred ministers.

## BOOKS

The Altar Book, designed as a sacramentary for the presider, also contains texts and chants for deacons. Deacons often use other books, especially for the gospel and the prayers of the people:

### (1) Book of the gospels
These books have a long history in the church. The Second Council of Nicaea in 787 decreed the veneration of gospel books (along with icons and crosses) as a symbol of Christ whose word the book contains. Before the Reformation (and to this day in the Roman Catholic Church), deacons received a book of the gospels at their ordination. This tradition became lost in England during the Reformation, replaced by the

giving of a New Testament. Since 1979 deacons of the Episcopal Church receive a complete Bible (given also to new bishops and priests). For deacons the gospel book has a liturgical significance different from the Bible. It is possible to restore the giving of a gospel book, as an extension of the gift of a Bible.

For the eucharistic lessons and gospels, the prayer book encourages the use of "a book or books of appropriate size and dignity" (BCP 406; BAS 183). This rubric has led to the publication in several versions of a book of the gospels, impressively bound in metal or leather. These contain gospel pericopes for Sundays, major feasts, and other occasions. Some editions of gospel books contain the entire text of the four gospels, with pericopes noted in the margins; these are more convenient, especially since a rubric permits the lengthening of any reading (BCP 888).

### (2) Prayers of the people
The history of liturgical books includes the *diaconicon* or diaconal, used only in eastern churches, containing all the deacon's parts in the liturgy. A western version of this book might consist of prayers of the people, compiled for weekly, seasonal, and occasional use.

## MUSIC

Liturgical chant elevates the text and brings out the meaning. Deacons may sing all the texts assigned to them, except for low-voiced parts such as the words at communion. The chants appointed in the Altar Book are based on traditional melodies. These chants are melodically simple and generous to singers of limited voice. Deacons should sing them in an unhurried and dignified manner, with respect for the rhythm and meaning of the words. The gospel, prayers of the people, and directions such as the dismissal are especially suitable for chanting.

*(1) Gospel*
The Altar Book provides two tones. Tone I is the Sarum form of an early melody. It consists of a reciting note with cadences or ending melodies at the *metrum* (major pause within a sentence), *punctum* (end of a sentence), question, and conclusion. Tone II dates from the late sixteenth century. It is simpler, without a cadence at the *metrum.* The people's responses are the same for both tones. Other traditional tones are also available, especially from the Ambrosian and Mozarabic rites, or deacons may compose their own tones based on simplified Anglican chant or Gregorian chant. One simple way to use gospel chant, or to introduce it to a congregation, is to sing only the announcement and the ending phrase, enabling the people to sing their responses (unaccompanied).

*(2) Prayers of the people*
As leaders or co-leaders of the general intercessions, deacons may sing all or part of these litanies. The Altar Book, Hymnal, and supplementary songbooks provide chants for the forms in the *Book of Common Prayer,* and for litanies based on them. The chants for Forms I and V (found in the *Hymnal 1982* at S 106 and S 109) are singable and appropriate for regular Sunday and festal use. Each form has two tones, derived from Gre-

gorian and Ambrosian sources. Other tones may be found in the Hymnal at S 107 (Form III), S 108 (Form IV), in its service music supplement at S 363 (Form VI), and in *Lift Every Voice and Sing II* (pages 247–251). A deacon sings the solemn biddings of Good Friday to the simple preface tone (given in the Altar Book). After each bidding the deacon may sing, "Let us kneel in silent prayer," and later, "Arise." The versicles and litanies in the daily office have their own chants. For other special and occasional litanies, a deacon may use traditional or modern formulas consisting of a reciting note with an ending cadence.

### (3) Dismissal

For dismissals during the year (except in Easter), the deacon sings a simple melody based on Gregorian chant (Hymnal S 174). For the Easter dismissal with two alleluias, the deacon sings the traditional Roman chant (Hymnal S 175). Those chants are widely known and beautiful, and generally preferable to the other selections provided in the Hymnal.

### (4) Processions

A deacon customarily begins a procession with a chant, to which the people respond. The Altar Book and Hymnal provide the music for "Let us go forth in peace" on Palm Sunday (Service Music Supplement S 342) and "The light of Christ" at the Easter Vigil (S 68). Other processions with diaconal chants (as at Candlemas) use similar music.

*(5) Exsultet*

Following ancient tradition, a deacon sings the paschal praises called the Exsultet (after the opening word in Latin) at the Easter Vigil. The chant given in the Altar Book comes from the Roman rite in the late Middle Ages. Differences in melodic treatment distinguish the introductory or "Rejoice" stanzas, with their lyric quality, from the formal blessing of the paschal candle, a recitation in the solemn preface tone. Other chants are available at online sites, including a simple chant in the Ambrosian preface tone and an ornate Beneventan chant used in southern Italy during the ninth through fourteenth centuries. Deacons of limited voice may simply sing the Exsultet as a monotone with slight inflections.

*(6) Prayers for the candidates*

For the litany in the baptismal rite, the Altar Book provides a chant from the Gregorian tradition.

BLESSINGS

The practice of pronouncing God's blessing on people, animals, and objects varies from place to place. Normally, in Anglican usage, formal blessings of the church are reserved to bishops and priests. This reservation applies mainly to the final blessing of the Eucharist, but local custom may extend it to other blessings both within and outside the liturgy. There is no restriction on informal blessings, which any person may give.

There is a trend to extend blessings to deacons in circumstances of need. Since their use of blessings may cause offense and lead to controversy, deacons need to exercise caution and seek advice and approval from the bishop or priest in charge.

Within the liturgy, deacons (and eucharistic ministers) sometimes bless children and others who do not receive communion. This practice may take the form of an actual blessing (with laying on of hands). Preferably, the deacon administers "spiritual communion" to those who do not receive the sacrament because of unwillingness or inability. (See chapter 3.)

Outside the liturgy, deacons frequently bless people during the exercise of diaconal ministry—as in hospitals, prisons, and other institutions. They also bless animals (in connection with the feast of St. Francis of Assisi) and objects such as crosses, mainly when no priest is available or when there is a need for additional ministers. Likewise, Roman Catholic deacons are allowed to bless sacramentals—objects such as rosaries, scapulars, icons, and crosses.

# 2

# CHRISTIAN INITIATION

THOSE WHO DESIRE to become a Christian pass from death to life and enter a new family in the sacrament of baptism. This pastoral, social, and liturgical passage takes place in the company of parents, godparents, sponsors, and the entire supporting Christian community. The role of deacons is to guide the candidates through darkness and perilous waters. Purged of sin and death, washed in the blood of the Lamb, and sealed by the Spirit, the new Christians follow deacons bearing the light of Christ into a new fellowship of brothers and sisters.

The church provides a short and a long form for Christian initiation: (1) *Holy Baptism* (suitable for both adults and children) and (2) the *Catechumenate,* ending in Holy Baptism (suitable only for adults or those mature enough to receive instruction). The church also provides a means for mature baptized persons to prepare to reaffirm their baptismal covenant (see chapter 6).

## HOLY BAPTISM

At a normal celebration of baptism, within the Eucharist, the deacon proclaims the gospel reading, leads intercessions, serves at the altar, and otherwise assists. Especially, the deacon:

*(1) Leads the procession to the font.*
The deacon bears the lighted paschal candle in the procession (unless it is already near the font) and continues to hold the candle during the baptism. At the Easter Vigil, the deacon usually hands the candle to the presider, who dips it into the water during the solemn blessing.

*(2) May lead the prayers for the candidates.*
Although the prayer book suggests a sponsor for the role (BCP 312; BAS 163), a deacon is also a proper litanist, especially when more than one deacon is present. A deacon may sing or say the petitions during the procession to the font.

*(3) May baptize, by immersion or pouring.*
After the presider has blessed the water, several different ministers may baptize different candidates. Each baptizer—presider, assisting priest, or deacon—is appropriately the one who has prepared, or helped to prepare, the candidate or parents.

*(4) Lights a candle from the paschal candle.*
The lighted candle is then handed to the newly baptized or, for infants and younger children, to a parent or godparent.

*(5) Leads the procession to the chancel.*
Bearing the paschal candle, the deacon leads the way back to the chancel for chrismation and reception of the newly baptized. The deacon then places the candle in its stand.

*(6) Helps to give communion to the newly baptized*
The reception of communion completes Christian initiation.

On a few exceptional occasions, a deacon may preside at baptism. If a bishop or priest is unavailable at the Easter Vigil, the Day of Pentecost, All Saints' Day or the Sunday following, or the feast of the Baptism of Our Lord, "the bishop may specially authorize a deacon to preside." The deacon must omit everything that follows the water baptism. Since this type of liturgy truncates Christian initiation, the church must supply the omitted parts later at a "public baptism at which a bishop or priest presides" (BCP 312). The Canadian church allows the deacon to include everything (BAS 163).

Parents and godparents "are to be instructed in the meaning of Baptism, in their duties to help the new Christian grow in the knowledge and love of God, and in their responsibilities as members of his Church" (BCP 298; BAS 150). In this preparation, deacons "have a special role as leaders of servant ministry" (BOS 161). The preparation of mature candidates properly occurs in the context of the catechumenate.

## THE CATECHUMENATE AND
## HOLY BAPTISM

The catechumenate is a period of integration and enlighten-
ment for adults who wish to become Christians. Details of the
period, including its liturgies, appear in *The Book of Occasional
Services 2003*. "Traditionally, the preparation of catechumens
is a responsibility of the bishop, which is shared with the presbyters, deacons, and appointed lay catechists of the diocese"
(BOS 114). The catechumenate consists of three stages leading up to baptism, followed by a fourth stage. It is normal for
deacons to minister in all four stages.

### (1) The pre-catechumenal period
Deacons may conduct inquiry classes and otherwise help inquirers decide whether they want to become Christians. A deacon may name the inquirers in the prayers of the people.

### (2) The catechumenate
Deacons may instruct catechumens in the Christian life,
prayer, and scripture. A sponsor (who may be a deacon) accompanies each catechumen through the process. Especially,
deacons lead and encourage catechumens in the care of the
poor, the weak, the sick, and the lonely, and show them that
in serving the helpless they serve Christ.

The stage begins with a rite of admission of catechumens,
in the midst of the Sunday liturgy. The sponsors mark a cross
on the foreheads of their catechumens. In the prayers of the
people, a deacon mentions the new catechumens by name.

During the stages of catechumenate and candidacy, at each formal teaching session the instructor—"whether bishop, priest, deacon, or lay catechist"—concludes by praying over the catechumens and then "by laying a hand individually on the head of each catechumen in silence" (BOS 119).

### (3) Candidacy for baptism

The stage normally coincides with Lent, with baptism at the Easter Vigil. (It may also occur in the incarnational cycle, with baptism on the feast of our Lord's Baptism.) The stage includes a rite of enrollment of candidates for baptism, after the creed on the first Sunday in Lent. The sponsors appear with their catechumens and may join them in signing the book of enrollment. For the prayers of the people, the deacon "or other person appointed" leads a special litany (BOS 124). On several Sundays during the stage, the candidates continue to come before the presider for special prayers and blessings and the laying on of hands. A deacon adds the names of candidates and sponsors to the prayers of the people.

In some places, following ancient practice, a deacon dismisses the catechumens and candidates after the homily (or Nicene Creed). In a typical formula, the deacon sings or says: "Let us pray in silence for the catechumens as they prepare to receive the wisdom of the Holy Spirit in baptism." After a period of silent prayer, the deacon continues: "Catechumens, go in peace." The catechumens leave with their sponsors and catechists to meet apart, for study and prayer, during the rest of the Eucharist. The sponsors and catechists return for communion.

When baptism occurs at the Great Vigil of Easter, as is the normal use, deacons function as usual. A deacon sponsoring a candidate also acts as sponsor. A deacon with a close relationship as either instructor or sponsor may baptize the candidate with water. Howard E. Galley's *Ceremonies of the Eucharist* provides a model form of the prayers of the people at baptism and confirmation (pp. 231–232). Paul V. Marshall suggests that the prayers for the candidates on Sunday "may well be followed without pause by intercessions and thanksgivings appropriate to the place and time."[6]

### (4) After baptism

The period after baptism, commonly called *mystagogia* (initiation into the mysteries or sacraments), extends through the fifty days of Easter. Less strictly defined than the catechumenate, the period involves integration into the life and worship of the church. Instructors and sponsors continue to help the new Christians. In the broadest sense, Christians live in *mystagogia* the rest of their lives, and even into death, as they continue to learn the mysteries of Christ's death and resurrection.

## EMERGENCY BAPTISM

Deacons sometimes need to administer baptism in an emergency, for a person near death or in some other crisis (BCP 313; BAS 164).

Baptism may include some persons beyond medical death. Even if a baby is stillborn or miscarried, or if a person has been declared dead, or appears dead, life may continue in a form we cannot recognize. As the gospels reveal in several stories, recently dead people are not necessarily dead. This is not an argument to baptize the long dead (like the Mormons), but to baptize those still in the process of dying, for whom earthly life remains a spiritual possibility. In our ignorance of God's reality, we do not know what is going on, or where they are, as they pass from life to death. Even time and space are different concepts for those crossing the river. So we dare to assume that God (or the angels) will correct the errors of our audacity.

If family members are present, ask their permission. If the person is unnamed, have the survivors give a name. Use whatever water is available, in whatever container. Using the given name, pour water on the person, saying,

> N., I baptize you in the Name of the Father, and of the Son, and of the Holy Spirit.

When the person may already have been baptized, the deacon administers baptism conditionally, saying,

> If you are not already baptized, N., I baptize you in the Name of the Father, and of the Son, and of the Holy Spirit.

Then all say the Lord's Prayer, and the deacon may add the prayer beginning with "Heavenly Father" (BCP 314).

Every baptism needs to be recorded somewhere. To record the baptism, the deacon informs the priest, pastor, or other minister in charge of the person's congregation. If the person has no congregation, or if the congregation is unknown, the deacon records the baptism in the deacon's home parish and sends the family a certificate of baptism.

3

# THE HOLY EUCHARIST

IN THE HOLY EUCHARIST, by who they are and what they do, deacons shed light on the paschal mystery of Christ and his church. They proclaim the good news of Christ's death and resurrection. They bring the needs, concerns, and hopes of the world into the marriage feast of the Lamb. They feed the hungry and give drink to the thirsty. By spreading the light of Christ in the darkness of the world, they serve both the people and the Lord.

Normally, one deacon takes the role of deacon, performing all the spoken and ceremonial functions of deacon. This person is commonly called *the deacon* or, in a celebration with several deacons, *the deacon of the mass.* (See the appendix for a summary of the deacon's functions in the Eucharist.)

Some places use two deacons, sharing duties in the Eucharist. They sit and stand one on each side of the presider. In a common arrangement, the deacon on the right of the presider reads the gospel and dismisses; the deacon on the left leads the prayers of the people and the confession of sin. At the preparation of the table and gifts, the left deacon helps the right, and the right deacon censes the presider and people. During the eucharistic prayer, both stand back a few steps; the left deacon turns pages, and the right deacon lifts the cup. Both receive communion from the presider, both give the wine (and bread, if necessary), and both consume the remaining wine and cleanse the vessels. Unless a bishop presides (see chapter 7 for details), other deacons serve mainly as ministers of communion.

## PREPARATION

All those with leadership roles prepare carefully for the celebration, praying and rehearsing the texts they are to sing or say. Deacons vest early, mark the books of the liturgy (unless others do this), remove their watches and jewelry, wash their hands, and oversee the preparation of others as necessary. They enforce a prayerful quiet in the vesting room. With others, they may say a prayer or office of preparation.

In some places a deacon or someone else, not necessarily ordained, stands at the ambo or other convenient place and makes what the prayer book calls "necessary announcements." These may include introducing the Eucharist of the day and rehearsing the people in a hymn or psalm refrain. (Announcements may take place before the service, after the Nicene Creed, before the preparation of the table, or at the end of the service.)

## THE ENTRANCE

The deacon carries the book of the gospels, held front forward and slightly elevated (but not obstructing the carrier's sight, which sometimes causes dizziness), and enters just ahead of the presider or, when these others are present, ahead of other deacons functioning liturgically, concelebrating priests and bishops, and presider. Without bowing or genuflecting, the deacon immediately places the book, closed and lying flat with the opening on the left, at the center of the altar (on the front or the back of the altar). When not carrying the book, the deacon enters at the right side of the presider, and they reverence the altar together. Where it is the custom, the deacon then kisses the altar (with hands joined) at the same time as the presider (who places hands flat on the altar).

When there are two deacons, one goes ahead with the gospel book, and the other walks either ahead of or on the left side of the presider. Without the gospel book, they walk on either side of the presider.

There are various ways of reverencing the altar, and every congregation has its own style. The normal reverence in Anglican practice is a deep bow from the waist before and after the liturgy. In some places it is the custom to bow whenever passing in front of the altar or the main cross, although such bows can be distracting and fussy. Where the reserved sacrament is present behind the altar, a single genuflection is common.

Censing the altar, if used, usually occurs during the entrance hymn or song, or sometimes during the song of praise

(*Gloria in excelsis* and the like). In its fullest form it takes place like this:

(1) The thurifer brings the censer to the presider. The deacon takes the boat and opens it, and the presider places incense on the coals.

(2) The deacon returns the boat to the thurifer, takes the censer, and passes it to the presider. The deacon places the top of the chains in the presider's left hand, the bottom of the chains in the right hand.

(3) Usually, the presider censes a free-standing altar by walking around it counter-clockwise, swinging the censer.[7] The deacon stands aside during the censing.

(4) The presider hands the censer back to the deacon, who returns it to the thurifer. Sometimes, thurifer and presider hand each other the censer directly, without using the deacon as an intermediary.

During the rest of the entrance rite, at the chair, the deacon may hold the Altar Book (or other printed material) for the presider, unless someone else does this.

The entrance rite may include several options:

(1) In the Penitential Order (often used during Lent), the deacon invites the people to confess and, after a period of silence, leads them in confession.

(2) In the Great Litany (often used on the First Sunday in Lent), the deacon may sing or say the petitions, kneeling, standing, or in procession.

(3) In the Order of Worship for the Evening, the deacon may light the candles and help with incense.

(4) During the fifty days of Easter, and perhaps on other Sundays, if the presider sprinkles the people with water (usually in place of or after the collect for purity), the deacon helps with water and sprinkler.

There are two other basic forms of gathering for liturgy, both derived from the early church:

### (1) Gathering as a body

As in a small or informal liturgy, the people gather as one body in the room of celebration. The deacon informally places the gospel book on the altar. Each person, including the liturgical ministers, bows separately on entering and takes a seat. The deacon may introduce the Eucharist of the day, make announcements, and conduct a rehearsal with a hymn or psalm refrain. After a brief period of silence, the presider stands and begins the liturgy, perhaps with the collect of the day.

### (2) Entering as a body

As on Palm Sunday or at the Easter Vigil (in many places), the people enter as one body into church, following their leaders. The deacon may organize the procession in the parish hall, make announcements, and conduct a rehearsal. The deacon may direct: "Let us go forth in peace" (with the people responding: "In the name of Christ. Amen."). Deacon and presider lead the way, with other ministers, and the liturgy begins as usual, perhaps with a shortened entrance rite.

## THE LITURGY OF THE WORD

After the collect of the day, while ministers read the lessons and chant the gradual psalm, all others sit. A deacon may monitor silence after each reading and give a discreet signal, or ring a gong or bell, when the silence is to end. If no qualified or competent reader is present, the deacon may read the lessons before the gospel, from the usual place.

### Proclamation of the Gospel

The deacon who is to read the gospel prepares carefully by studying the text, practicing it aloud, and absorbing it in prayerful meditation.

In a simple weekday liturgy, the deacon may read the gospel without adornment, perhaps preceded by a blessing. On Sundays and major feasts, the assembly adorns the gospel with signs of honor. Because the proclamation of the gospel marks the high point of the Liturgy of the Word, its ceremony is often long and elaborate. Two lights accompany the book of the gospels to the place of reading. Some congregations use incense, regularly or occasionally. In some places or on solemn occasions, the deacon chants the gospel.

The gospel ceremony typically takes place in this way. After the second reading, the assembly observes a period of silence. After the silence, or toward the end of a sequence hymn, the deacon and others rise to prepare for the gospel procession. The candlebearers take up their torches. The thurifer brings the censer, if used, to the presider, as at the entrance.

The blessing of the deacon is an old custom. The deacon bows low and quietly asks the presider: "Father *or* Mother, give me your blessing," a rough translation of *Iube, domine, benedicere.* The presider makes the sign of the cross or, in a scriptural form of blessing, lays one or both hands on the deacon's head. Meanwhile, the presider says a blessing.

Two blessings are suggested here. The first, traditional in the western church, is from the current *Missale Romanum:*

> The Lord be in your heart and on your lips, that you may worthily proclaim his gospel: In the name of the Father, and of the Son, and of the Holy Spirit.

The second, a paraphrase of Luke 4:18, is from the Bobbio Missal reflecting Gallican practices in the seventh and eighth centuries:

> May the Spirit of the Lord be upon you as you bring good news to the poor.

The deacon responds "Amen" and turns to join the procession. (The blessing normally takes place before the procession. For reasons of space and movement, it may take place during the procession or at the end of it.)[8]

The deacon goes to the altar, bows low, and takes up the book. Preceded by (thurifer and) candlebearers, and perhaps by someone to hold the book during the reading, the deacon holds the book slightly elevated and walks reverently to the place of reading. Traditionally, a cross is not carried in the procession, since in this proclamation the gospel book is the primary symbol of Christ. During the procession, in some places, the choir or people sing alleluias or (in Lent) some psalm verses, known as the tract. In places without these chants, the people finish the sequence hymn. The people turn toward the deacon or even, space permitting, gather around.

The procession moves to a prominent place. "It is desirable that the Lessons be read from a lectern or pulpit, and that the Gospel be read from the same lectern, or from the pulpit, or from the midst of the congregation" (BCP 406; BAS 183). Like other lists in the prayer book, the first option is preferred. Use of a lectern (sometimes called ambo) or pulpit for the entire Liturgy of the Word makes it possible for all to see and hear. It also emphasizes the unity of the word of God. The second option (pulpit) assumes that the previous lessons have been read from the pulpit. The third option (midst of the congregation) reflects a practice dating from the 1950s, during the postwar wave of liturgical renewal, emphasizing Christ proclaimed in the world. Especially in a large space, the place of proclamation should enable all the people to see and hear the deacon.

At a lectern (ambo) or pulpit, the deacon places the book on the stand and opens it. In the midst of the congregation, the deacon hands the book to someone else, who holds it open.

In the Canadian church, following an old custom, the deacon then greets the people with "The Lord be with you." This greeting, with hands extended, is sometimes used by deacons in Episcopal churches. Having received blessing from the presider, the deacon gives blessing to the people, and the people give blessing back to the deacon.

The deacon announces the reading, making a sign of the cross with the right thumb on the opening word of the gospel, forehead, lips, and breast. If incense is used, the deacon then censes the open book with three swings—center, left, right. Hands joined, the deacon sings or says the gospel in a slow and stately manner, looking at the text. At the end of the reading, the deacon pauses briefly, looks at the people, and concludes: "The gospel of the Lord." It is unnecessary to elevate the book, although this is often done. The deacon then kisses the opening word, praying quietly: "May the words of the gospel wipe away our sins." (If the presider is a bishop, the deacon omits the kiss and brings the book directly to the bishop to kiss.)

Ancient custom, still observed in some places, called for the deacon to chant the gospel. If the deacon sings at least the opening and closing formulas, the people are able to sing their response. Today, sadly, few deacons sing the entire gospel; perhaps it is fairer to say that few places let them sing it. If God has given the gift of song to a deacon, however, the assembly has the right to enjoy it for the glory of God, at least on great feasts such as Christmas and Easter.

Unless the deacon leaves the book of the gospels on a lectern or pulpit, or hands it to someone to bring back, the deacon takes the closed book and leads the procession back to the altar. The deacon places the book on the altar (where it remains until the kiss of peace) or on a side table. If the presider is a bishop, the deacon first brings the book open or closed to the bishop (who is perhaps on the way to preach), who venerates the book with a kiss and may use the book to bless the people with the sign of the cross.[9]

A deacon who is to preach remains in place, or goes to a lectern or pulpit, while the others return to their places. The deacon may keep the gospel book or give it to someone else to bring back. It is better to gesture (palms down) than to ask the people to sit. When everyone has settled down, the deacon begins immediately, without announcements, invocation, prayer, joke, or cheery greeting such as "Good morning." The deacon concludes simply or with a doxology. After the homily, there may be a brief period of silence. The deacon may then lead the people by beginning the Nicene Creed.

## LEADING THE GENERAL INTERCESSIONS

Near the end of the creed, the deacon goes to a suitable place for (announcements and) the prayers of the people.[10]

The leaders of the general intercessions are deacons or other baptized persons. By leading or participating in leading these prayers, deacons fulfill their ordination role as those who interpret to the church the needs, concerns, and hopes of the world. Other baptized persons, whether leading or praying as part of the assembly, fulfill their role as those who share in the priesthood of Christ. Those who lead suggest topics and invite the people to pray; the people offer petitions to God.

Although deacons are the preferred leaders, it is common for other baptized persons to lead the prayers. Deacons and other baptized persons can share leadership in several different ways:

(1) the deacon gives the introductory sentence, and others bid prayer;

(2) the deacon and others alternate biddings and petitions;

(3) others bid prayer, and the deacon invites the people to respond (as with "let us pray to the Lord"); or

(4) others read special intentions before or during the
prayers, and the deacon bids prayer.

If all who lead prayer also minister to those in need in the
church and the world, their leadership in prayer will convey
authority.

The prayer book provides several models of intercessions:
the form for Rite One (BCP 328–330) and the six forms suggested for general use (BCP 383–393). The Canadian church
provides nineteen models (BAS 110–128). All these are presented as forms for possible use and even as examples, not as
standard forms required for regular use. The prayer book permits wide freedom: "Any of the forms which follow may be
used. Adaptations or insertions suitable to the occasion may
be made" (BCP 383). The Canadian book is even clearer:
"These forms . . . ought not to become the standard forms used
in a parish, but should be adapted with imagination to meet
the needs of the local Church" (BAS 177). The liturgical leaders in a congregation may change the forms, compose new
forms, or adapt other forms for every Sunday and feast, the
seasons of the church year, or special occasions.

To compose or adapt the intercessions, the deacon may
work with other persons. It is desirable to have someone skilled
in literary composition do the actual drafting. In composing
intercessions, drafters follow six principles:

*(1) Include six categories*
The six categories of subject matter are: (1) the church, (2) the
nation and all in authority, (3) the world, (4) the local community, (5) those in need, and (6) the dead (BCP 359 and
383; BAS 190). Cover these topics in full on Sundays and

major feasts, and condense them on weekdays and other occasions.

*(2) Cover general topics*
The prayers ask God's mercy on all those in need in the church
and the world. Use specific names and local concerns with re-
straint. Except on occasions such as weddings and funerals, it
is better to announce special intentions before the intercessions—and then briefly and selectively. It is an ancient custom
to include the given name of the bishop in the formal biddings.

*(3) Emphasize intercession*
At its heart intercession asks God to relieve needs, remedy concerns, and fulfill hopes. Although prayer book Forms II and VI
include brief thanksgivings, the emphasis should be on intercession. It is better to leave thanksgiving to other parts of the
liturgy, or to the daily office.

*(4) Let the people pray*
Intercessions are prayers of the people, not of the leader. When
deacons lead, they act as heralds or messengers, announcing
topics and calling for prayer. In the early or classic type of intercession, a deacon addresses the people, reminding them of
topics, and the people respond with spoken or silent prayer.
In several forms in the prayer book, a leader invokes God in
terms such as "Father, we pray. . . . " Addressing God directly is
suitable mainly when other baptized persons lead the prayers;
they are exercising a priestly function through prayer. Prayer in
which the leader does most of the praying, while the people lis-

ten, or while their response is a single "Amen," removes the people from their priestly role as those who offer petitions. Even Rite One, with its long prayer "for the whole state of Christ's Church and the world," allows the alternative use of litanies.

### (5) Keep the biddings short and simple

Brief biddings are easy to follow and help the people to grasp the topic. It also helps if all the biddings are of the same liturgical format and follow a common grammatical structure. Biddings may begin with a formula such as "For [persons or concerns]" or "That [intention]." These may be combined as "For [persons or concerns], that [intention]." Biddings may end abruptly (mainly when sung) or, to prompt the response, with a cue such as "let us pray to the Lord." A sensible number is four or five biddings on weekdays, and six to twelve on Sundays and major feasts. Petitions addressed to God should also be short and simple.

### (6) Keep the responses short and uniform

Long responses and ones that change from petition to petition require the people to read from a book or piece of paper. Short, unchanging responses allow them to look up and see the leader and each other, the altar, a cross, an icon, and other aids to prayer. They are free to hold hands, raise them in prayer, and even move about (as in a circle).

The presider, deacon, or drafting committee may also adapt or compose the brief invitation and the concluding collect.

These usually reflect the occasion, season, or day. The presider needs a copy of the text.

There are three main places to lead the prayers:

*(1) At the lectern or pulpit*
The deacon faces the people, emphasizing the role of messenger addressing the people. This place is common in the western church.

*(2) In the midst of or at the head of the congregation*
The deacon may begin by facing the people (or by facing away from the altar) during the invitation to pray. After the invitation or opening phrase, the deacon turns to face the altar, or liturgical east, emphasizing prayer oriented toward the rising sun. This place is common in the eastern church.

*(3) At the deacon's seat or normal place to stand*
This place, emphasizing the centered unity of the congregation, works best in spaces arranged antiphonally or in a circle.

The choice of a place should suit the worship space and the needs of the congregation. The people may remain standing at their seats, pray in procession from the word space to the altar space, or form a circle around the altar. They may focus on an icon or some other point of prayer. The presider may stand on one side of the assembly (altar or liturgical east), or at the other side, or at the chair. The deacon may stand on the opposite side, or among the people, or at an ambo. The place should be permanent and not change from Sunday to Sunday.

The prayers of the people take place in this way. After the presider's invitation, the deacon may read, or arrange for others to read, special intentions of the diocese and the congregation. These may include the Anglican and diocesan cycles of prayer, baptismal days, wedding anniversaries, the sick, the dead, and names and concerns of the local community. For this purpose, leaders may use a large notebook or permanent book of weekly remembrances, with blank pages for names. It is better to concentrate on a few intentions than to overwhelm the congregation with long lists.

After the special intentions, the leader may invite the people to recall their daily prayers and offer their own names and concerns silently or aloud. After giving them a little time, the deacon or other leader begins the formal biddings.

While singing or saying the biddings, the deacon keeps hands joined (when facing the people at the lectern) or extends them in the *orans* or prayer gesture (when facing *ad orientem* from the congregation). To hold the prayer gesture, the deacon may need to memorize the biddings, or someone else may hold a book containing the text. Alternatively, when facing east the deacon may keep hands joined or, in a gesture from Orthodox practice, hold the end of the stole in three fingers of the right hand.

When the intercessions take the form of a litany, it is desirable to sing them. The leader sings either the whole bidding or the ending phrase. If necessary, someone else sings the ending phrase. The people sing their response either in unison or in harmony. They may overlap a response such as "Lord, have mercy" with the preceding bidding and hum during the following bidding.

At the end, perhaps after a period of silence, the presider extends hands and concludes with a collect or doxology.

### Confession and Peace

If the people confess their sins just before the peace, the deacon (in the same place) says the invitation and, after a period of silence long enough to recollect sins, bows deeply and begins the confession. For the absolution, the deacon rises and makes the sign of the cross with the rest of the congregation.

If the people are slow to rise for the peace, the deacon may gesture for them to stand (palms up). After the presider has given the peace, the deacon may announce, with hands joined, "Offer one another a sign of peace," or give a similar direction (singing it, if the presider has sung the peace sentence). (The deacon's sentence, permitted under the rubric for announcements, is a translation of *Offerte vobis pacem* in the Roman and Ambrosian rites.) Then the deacon receives the sign of peace from the presider, according to local custom, and gives it to others nearby. The formal greeting in the western church is a light embrace cheek to cheek.

Before the preparation of the table, the deacon or someone else may make other necessary announcements. These should be brief and help the liturgy move to the next action.

## THE LITURGY OF THE SACRAMENT

As in the ancient church, deacons prepare the table and the bread and wine. The common name of this action is the *Offertory*, from the people's offerings of bread and wine and other gifts. A more accurate name, covering the entire action, is *Preparation of the Table and Gifts.*

## PREPARATION OF THE TABLE AND GIFTS

When the prayer book speaks of what the deacon does in the offertory or preparation, it uses domestic language, words of kitchen and dining room, food and drink, and a festive table where people gather to eat. A deacon "make[s] ready the Table for the celebration, preparing and placing upon it the bread and cup of wine," to which it is customary "to add a little water" (for sobriety, originally) (BCP 407; see BAS 183).

When the prayer book speaks of what the presider and people do, it uses temple language, words of sacrifice, offering, and altar. Members of the assembly bring to the deacon "the people's offerings of bread and wine, and money or other gifts." These "are presented and placed on the Altar" (BCP 333, 361; see BAS 192).

To describe the action another way, in the Liturgy of the Sacrament deacons and other liturgical helpers function as table waiters, while the presider functions as a ministerial priest and the people as members of a sacred priesthood. Waiters wait on table, priests offer sacrifice. Working together, deacons and ministerial priests set free and enable the entire assembly to act at the highest level of baptismal role, offering praise and thanksgiving and eating the messianic banquet, as all share in the royal and eternal priesthood of Christ.

Throughout the preparation, the presider remains at the presidential chair, a model of quiet prayer. Helped by others, the deacon stands at the table, carrying out an action as traditional and formal as the *sadō* or Japanese tea ceremony. The following description assumes a freestanding table, with deacon facing the people across it, facing west; for a table against the wall, facing east, the deacon will have to make appropriate adjustments in these directions. The preparation requires four distinct steps:

## (1) Prepare the table

The deacon or a server brings the corporal and the vessels to the table and places them on the right side. The deacon spreads the corporal in the center and arranges the empty paten (plate) and chalice (cup) on the right.

The rubrics require the table to be "spread with a clean white cloth during the celebration" (BCP 406). In some places members of the altar guild still spread the corporal before the celebration, with vested chalice on top, a practice with roots in the Middle Ages. As the rubric indicates, it is preferable to spread the corporal when it is needed, emphasizing the preparation of the table as a distinct action beginning the Liturgy of the Sacrament. Without a chalice already on the table, the veil and burse no longer fill a symbolic role; if used, they should be removed before the vessels are brought to the table.

The corporal (from Latin *corpus* or body, because it collects spilled fragments of the body of Christ) was originally what we now call the "fair linen," a large white cloth covering the entire top of the table. This practice may still be followed, with the table left completely bare until the preparation and a large white cloth spread as both corporal and fair linen.

The typical corporal is a square white cloth with a cross sewn on the center of the bottom edge, folded in nine squares. The deacon places it on the center of the table, folded with the exposed edge on the right, and unfolds it carefully in this order: center to left, center to right, center to top, and center to bottom. The deacon then pulls the corporal by two corners so that the bottom edge (with the cross) lines up with the edge of the table. If the corporal does not unfold in the correct order, the deacon may either unfold it as is or fold it correctly and start over. It is desirable to avoid unsightly flurries of cloth being rearranged. (If the problem occurs frequently, the deacon should work with the altar guild to correct it.)

The prayer book requires "only one chalice on the Altar, and, if need be, a flagon of wine from which additional chalices may be filled after the Breaking of the Bread" (BCP 407; see BAS 184). The reason for one chalice lies in scriptural and traditional evidence of one cup (and one bread) as a sign of unity. The deacon sets the plate and cup on the table, in one of two places: (1) on the right, alongside the corporal, or (2) on the corporal. Both places are commonly used. My preference is to place the vessels alongside the corporal until they are ready, containing bread and wine, to be placed on the corporal.

In some congregations, members bring up the bread already on a plate, or loaves in a basket, to be used on the table. If this is to happen, the deacon prepares the table with only a cup for the wine.

The deacon uses the purificator (cloth napkin) to wipe the inside of the cup and then places it on the right, alongside the corporal. The pall (a stiff square card covered with white linen) goes to the right of the purificator. When necessary, the pall is used to protect the wine from insects and dirt. The deacon places it bottom up, with one edge slightly over the near edge of the table, so that it can be picked up easily and turned over to cover the cup.

### (2) Receive the gifts

The deacon receives the offerings from members of the congregation and places them on the table.

The prayer book provides for "the deacon or celebrant" to receive the offerings (BCP 333, 361; BAS 192), but the deacon (as the one mentioned first) usually handles this function. To receive the gifts, the deacon (perhaps with a server) stands either behind the table or in front of it, at the steps, facing the people. The prayer book does not specify the location, and it is common in the Episcopal Church for the deacon to stand behind the altar. The Canadian church requires the deacon to receive the gifts "before the altar" (BAS 192).

Members of the congregation bring, in this order: special gifts (such as food for the hungry), money, and bread and wine. They present the bread and wine directly to the deacon (or presider), who places them on the table. Someone else may handle the special gifts and money. Special gifts go nearby, money nearby or on the right corner of the table (to be removed just before the eucharistic prayer), bread and wine to the right of the plate and cup, off the corporal. (In some places the bread and wine arrive first, and the money comes last, after an anthem or hymn, to be blessed by the presider. Where this happens, the deacon goes ahead and receives the bread and wine and prepares them.) Finally, the deacon goes behind the table (unless already there) to prepare the gifts.

*(3) Prepare the gifts*
The deacon prepares the gifts by putting them in their proper vessels, bread in a plate and other containers, wine in a cup and other containers.

Standing behind the table, at the center, the deacon puts the bread on the plate. This may be in the form of several large wafers, or of a large host and many small wafers, or of one or more loaves. Where there are a large number of wafers, some may have to go in another container.

The deacon (or a second deacon, if present) pours sufficient wine in the cup and in any flagons, decanters, or other containers to remain on the table. The deacon (or second deacon) adds a little water to the wine in the cup and other containers. While pouring the water, the deacon may pray quietly:

> By the mystery of this water and wine,
> may we come to share in the divinity of Christ,
> who humbled himself to share in our humanity.

The theology behind the prayer, used in the Roman rite, dates from the early church and reflects the Orthodox concept of *theosis,* the mystical union of God and humanity.[11] Servers usually help by bringing a cruet of water and taking away unneeded vessels. There is no reason for the water to be presented with the gifts or for the presider to bless the water.

*(4) Place the gifts*
The deacon places the vessels on the corporal. The plate with the bread goes on the left, the cup of wine on the right. The reasons for this positioning are both ancient and practical. In the early church, the bishop was often old, the bread plate

large, and the wine bowl heavy. At certain points the bishop raised the bread, sometimes with help, and a deacon, usually much younger, raised the wine bowl. Deacons also needed to keep insects from the wine bowl—hence the large fans still used ceremonially in some eastern liturgies, and the pall or folded corporal in western liturgies.

Today, placing the vessels side by side makes them fully visible to the congregation and emphasizes the centrality of worship around one altar. In places where the presider prefers the late medieval arrangement of chalice behind paten, the deacon must set the table in that manner.

Ciboria, flagons, and other containers, with lids removed, usually go on either side, bread to the left and wine to the right, allowing the people to see the plate and cup. If many, they may have to be placed off the corporal. Unless insects are a threat, all vessels should be open and uncovered throughout the eucharistic prayer.

When all is ready, the deacon steps aside (to the right and back), and the bishop or priest comes to the altar. In some congregations this is the point where plates of money arrive, and the presider may wish to elevate them while everyone sings a doxology or other song.

The rite of censing (if used) helps the assembly to lay aside earthly cares and, with angels and saints, gather prayerfully for the mystery about to take place. The deacon helps the presider, who puts incense on the coals, censes the bread and wine, and circles the altar counterclockwise, swinging the censer. The presider hands the censer to the deacon. The deacon then censes the presider and the people, either with three swings for each group or walking among them and swinging continuously. It is customary to give two swings to a priest and three to a bishop, or the deacon may cense groups of people as a body and treat bishops, priests, and other baptized persons as equals. The deacon bows deeply before and after censing persons and objects. The deacon then hands the censer to the thurifer. (In some places, after the deacon has censed the presider, the thurifer censes the people.)

For the lavabo or washing of hands, normally a server (but sometimes by necessity the deacon) goes to the presider with a towel over the left arm, a bowl in the left hand, and a small pitcher of water in the right hand. Although in western tradition only the presider need receive the lavabo, deacons and other ministers of communion who have exchanged the peace may also wash their hands, without being conspicuous, to reduce the risk of spreading disease.

Someone takes away the money or other gifts. The deacon or a server places the Altar Book on the left side of the altar, with ribbons in place and open to the beginning of the eucharistic prayer. The concelebrating priests and bishops (if any) and deacons take their places.

Before beginning the eucharistic prayer, the presider may lift the bread and cup. The presider is also likely to rearrange the vessels, napkins, leaflets, and books on the altar, sometimes slightly, sometimes to an entirely new configuration. The deacon can anticipate most of this shuffling by arranging the table as the presider prefers. Otherwise, there is little to do but stand aside and look on.

## THE EUCHARISTIC PRAYER

The arrangement of ministers at any altar depends on the location of the table, the space around it, and the customs of the congregation. This is one pattern, preferred if possible.

Inconspicuous but ready, the deacon stands on the right side of the presider and two or three steps back, hands joined. Another deacon, if present, takes the same position on the left. The right deacon attends to the cup, the left deacon the book. A single deacon stands on the right and moves as needed to turn pages and lift the cup, unless someone else turns pages.

If the presider bows at "Holy, holy, holy," the deacon also bows deeply, rising at the first "Hosanna in the highest." It is not necessary to make the sign of the cross at "Blessed is he [or the one]," unless the presider makes the sign. If the cup is covered with a pall, the deacon removes it for the words concerning the wine, the epiclesis, and the final doxology (unless the presider prefers to do this). At the beginning of the final doxology, the deacon steps to the altar and lifts the cup, while the presider lifts the bread (close together and at the same height), replaces it after "Amen," and steps back. Then, while the presider bows or genuflects, the deacon imitates this motion. (Some presiders prefer to lift both the bread and the cup. The deacon needs to remain in place.)

When incense is used during the eucharistic prayer, a thurifer normally does the censing. On occasion, another deacon (if available) may stand in front of the altar and swing the censer continuously. It is customary to cense the sacrament with three double swings during the final doxology.

In each eucharistic prayer, the invitation to the memorial acclamation is addressed to God and thus is part of the presider's role. Because the intercessions in Prayer D (Canadian Prayer 6) are in the form of prayer, the presider normally says them, although the bishop may give special permission for deacons to say them. On an occasion such as the feast of All Saints or the Sunday after, the deacon or someone else may read a list of the parish dead in that place in Prayer D.

Where it is the custom for the congregation to extend hands during the Lord's Prayer, or where the presider gives permission or encouragement, the deacon also may use the *orans* gesture. In this way the deacon helps to lead the people in outward signs of prayer.

THE BREAKING OF THE BREAD
The presider breaks the loaf or large wafer in two and prays silently. During the period of silence, or later, the deacon may pray quietly:

> Wisdom has built her house,
> she has mixed her wine, she has set her table.
> Glory to you, O God, for ever.[12]

While the presider (assisted by concelebrating priests and bishops) continues to break the bread, during the fraction anthem, the deacon and others bring additional plates and cups, as needed, to the altar and fill the cups from the flagons. "In the absence of a sufficient number of priests, deacons may assist in the Bread-breaking" (BOS 17).

## THE COMMUNION

When the presider, lifting the bread, says the invitation to communion, the deacon lifts the cup, showing it to the people. It is not necessary to lift all the vessels containing consecrated bread and wine.

The manner of giving communion varies from place to place. Here is a typical pattern. Before the presider eats the bread and drinks the wine, the deacon quietly says the words of administration. Since all the people of God *receive* communion, not *take* it, in some places deacons administer communion to the presider. The presider then gives the body and blood of Christ to the deacon, and then both give communion to other deacons and concelebrating priests and bishops. The other liturgical ministers then communicate, and after them the rest of the people. In some places, despite the rubric requiring the ministers to receive communion before the people, they receive it last; they should at least receive it from one another.

Normally, deacons and eucharistic ministers give the cup, following the presider (and other priests) along a line of communicants, or standing at a station. After saying the communion sentence, the deacon allows each communicant time to say "Amen" before giving the cup. The deacon may have to help children, older persons, and others grasp the cup and guide it to their mouth. Infants may have to suck wine from the deacon's or a parent's finger.

"When several deacons or priests are present, some may administer the Bread and others the Wine" (BCP 408; see BAS 666). Under canon law, eucharistic ministers may give bread or wine. There should be sufficient ministers and stations for communion to take place slowly and reverently. Deacons may fill cups from flagons and otherwise help the other ministers. The presider, if elderly or ill or simply in need of rest and prayer, may sit down and let others give communion.

Deacons (and eucharistic ministers) are sometimes expected to give a blessing to a non-communicating child or adult. This blessing falls under the rubric of spiritual communion, whereby a person who is unable to eat and drink the sacrament receives "all the benefits of Communion" (BCP 457). The blessing may take this form: Laying a hand on the child's head or shoulder, the deacon says the sentence of administration or "May God bless you and keep you." The same rubric applies to adults who cannot consume the bread or the wine. Saying the sentence, the deacon may hold the sacrament before the person or lay a hand on the person's head or shoulder.

Because of communicable illness or other sound reason, some persons prefer to receive the sacrament "in both kinds simultaneously, in a manner approved by the bishop" (BCP 408). The manner usually means intinction, either by the minister or by the communicant, dipping a piece of bread in the wine and then placing it on the communicant's tongue.

If not already seated, the presider goes to the chair after communion. Deacons and eucharistic visitors take bread and wine for the communion of the sick and other absent persons. Eucharistic visitors come to the altar, and deacons give them bread and wine from the remaining elements (never from the reserved sacrament), usually in kits containing a pyx and a bottle. A prayer or statement of purpose accompanies the action. *Enriching Our Worship 2* suggests these or similar words:

In the name of this congregation, I send you forth
bearing these holy gifts, that those to whom you go
may share with us in the communion of Christ's body
and blood. We who are many are one body, because
we all share one bread, one cup. (EOW2 62)

Or the deacon may simply say:

Go in peace, bearing holy gifts for holy people.

(For information on the selection, training, licensing, and ministry of eucharistic visitors, with a liturgy for distributing communion, see BOS 322–326 and EOW2 59–63.)

If some of the sacrament needs to be reserved, the deacon
takes the remaining bread (and wine) to the tabernacle or aumbry (from Latin *almarium* or cupboard). In some places the
taking and reserving of the remaining sacrament occur later.

Cleaning up after communion—the ablutions (from Latin
*abluere* or wash away)—is a practical and unobtrusive activity.
At the Ordination of Deacons, the rubrics say, "If the remaining Elements are not required for the Communion of the absent, it is appropriate for the deacons to remove the vessels
from the Altar, consume the remaining Elements, and cleanse
the vessels in some convenient place" (BCP 555; see BAS 184).
These three actions—removing, consuming, and cleansing—
take place usually immediately after communion (or during
the postcommunion prayer or closing hymn) and usually in
the order given. The prayer book also permits them to occur
after the dismissal (BCP 409; BAS 184).

The deacon supervises the cleaning operation in several
stages:

(1) The deacon reserves the bread and wine needed for communion of the sick, putting them in a tabernacle, aumbry, or other container.

(2) The deacon and others, as needed, take the remaining bread and wine to a side table or another room.

(3) The deacon folds the corporal back into its original shape and removes it from the altar. Someone removes the Altar Book, unless the presider is to lead the postcommunion prayer from the altar.

(4) The deacon and others consume what remains. After eating the bread, they empty the crumbs into the cups and drink the wine. If there is a great amount of wine, they may dispose of it reverently, by pouring it down a *piscine* (drain to the ground outside) or *sacrarium* (sink for washing used vessels, with drain to the ground) or directly onto the ground. When only a little wine remains, the deacon may consume it at the altar before removing the vessels.

(5) The deacon and others rinse the cups with a little water, which they drink or pour down the *piscine* or *sacrarium*. They wipe the cups, plates, and other containers with purificators or cloth napkins.

## THE DISMISSAL

The deacon goes to the presider's side, or nearby, for the blessing and dismissal. In Lent, if the presider uses a formal prayer over the people, the deacon first faces the people and sings or says, "Bow down before the Lord" (BOS 24). Hands joined, facing the people, the deacon sings or says the dismissal. The prayer book assumes that the dismissal comes immediately after the blessing, as two parts of a single action. If local custom inserts a hymn between the two, with all the liturgical ministers retiring to the front door, the deacon should still remain in front of the people or return to the front to give the dismissal.

The prayer book gives four formulas for the dismissal, without permission for another formula. Deacons may use them interchangeably or vary them by theme and season. Despite these choices, the most common dismissal remains: "Go in peace to love and serve the Lord." During the fifty days of Easter (and at no other time), the deacon adds "alleluia, alleluia" to the dismissal.

In some places, with the approval of the bishop or presider, seasonal and occasional dismissals are used. These should be brief and simple, avoiding hortatory or sermonizing material. Several dismissals in common use are:

*Advent:*
Go in peace to prepare the way of the Lord.

*Christmas and Epiphany:*
Go in the peace of the Word made flesh.

*Lent:*
Go in peace to prepare for the paschal feast.

*Easter:*
Go in the peace of the risen Christ, alleluia, alleluia.

The deacon and presider (kiss the altar and) bow deeply before the altar and go out in the same order as they came in. In some celebrations, usually small and informal, they may disperse without further ceremony. Unless going to a liturgical celebration in another place, the deacon does not carry the gospel book out of the assembly.

## OTHER FORMS OF CELEBRATION

A community assembled regularly as church celebrates the normal eucharistic liturgy, typically with priest, deacon, cantor and other musicians, readers, eucharistic ministers, servers, and congregation. Deacons also serve in other forms of celebration:

### (1) Eucharist with a bishop
See chapter 7 for details.

### (2) Concelebration
In a form used mainly at ordinations and other diocesan liturgies, and sometimes at large parish liturgies, additional priests and bishops join the presider at the altar or nearby during the eucharistic prayer. The concelebrating priests and bishops need

to be careful to give the deacons room to help with book and cup. Rather than moving aside from time to time, which is distracting, they may leave a gap on either side of the presider or remain back in a semicircle until they step forward to join in the breaking of the bread.

### (3) Less formal or house liturgies

Many congregations hold informal liturgies in homes, schools, family settings, picnics, and the like. A few small congregations lacking a church building meet regularly in houses or other informal places. Wherever they take place, informal liturgies ought to include a diversity of ministries. The nature of the gathering usually calls for careful reduction or alteration in ceremony, without losing the spirit of the liturgy.

### (4) Communion service with the reserved sacrament

A communion service led by a deacon, using the reserved sacrament, includes most of the normative liturgy except the people's offering of bread and wine, eucharistic prayer, and breaking of the bread. Both bread and wine should be administered. Formerly (and mistakenly) called a *deacon's mass,* the liturgy is intended for use in an emergency, when a priest is suddenly unavailable. The bishop must authorize the service, and many bishops forbid it entirely. Its use as a regular liturgy in a congregation, over a long time, distorts the nature of ministry and worship and deprives the congregation of the full expression of *ecclesia* in that place. The 1979 *Book of Common Prayer* outlines the rite on page 408; the Canadian church makes no provision for the service.

*(5) Giving the reserved sacrament*
As part of their normal ministry, deacons use brief liturgies to give the sacrament to two kinds of communicants:

(1) *Those unable to attend the Eucharist for a long time:* Deacons use the form for Communion under Special Circumstances (BCP 396; BAS 257).

(2) *The sick:* Deacons use the form for Communion under Special Circumstances. They may include this form as part of Ministration to the Sick (BCP 457; BAS 556; see also the material in *Enriching Our Worship 2: Ministry with the Sick or Dying*).

In both circumstances, whenever possible, the deacon should administer both bread and wine.

4

# THE DAILY OFFICE

AT THEIR BAPTISM all Christians enter a life of prayer, both private and communal. Deacons swear at their ordination to "be faithful in prayer, and in the reading and study of the Holy Scriptures" (BCP 544; BAS 655). They fulfill this duty especially in the daily offices of Morning Prayer and Evening Prayer. Deacons function in these offices on four levels:

*(1) Private*
If prayer in community is unavailable, deacons pray the daily office privately, often in a simplified form. Their private prayer is united spiritually with the daily prayer of all other Christians, whether they pray in private or gather with others.

*(2) Family*
Daily prayer in families and other close groups lies at the heart of the Christian life. A parent, child, or someone else may lead, and different persons may read lessons, lead litanies, and say

prayers. The family group may shorten or alter the office to make it simple and easy to pray.

### (3) Sung or said office

When a community sings or says the daily office in church or elsewhere, it is unnecessary to follow distinctions of order. A deacon may function as officiant or assistant, or simply as a member of the assembly. In the absolution, an officiating deacon or other baptized person substitutes "us" for "you" and "our" for "your" (BCP 42, 63, 80, 117; BAS 46). Similarly, the officiant alters a blessing at the end of Worship for the Evening (BCP 114). As assistant to a bishop or priest, a deacon may read the gospel when it is a lesson and sing the intercessions and dismissal.

### (4) Solemn office

Solemnity in the daily office, commonly known as the cathedral or popular office, includes the use of diverse ministries in order (bishop or priest, deacons, cantor, readers, acolytes), distinctive vestments (copes, dalmatics, stoles), processions, chant, candle-lighting, and incense. Communities sometimes sing Morning Prayer solemnly on Sundays and feasts. More commonly, they sing Evensong solemnly on Saturdays and Sundays, feasts and their eves, and special occasions. One or two deacons wear the dalmatic, help with incense, sing the gospel (if used), chant the litany, and dismiss the people. Two attending deacons assist a bishop who presides (or is present), helping with mitre and crozier. At the *Phos hilaron* or candle-lighting hymn the presider censes the altar by walking around it.

The deacon or a server then censes the officiant and
the people. (If other clergy are present in the
sanctuary, they are censed collectively along with the
officiant. The bishop of the diocese, however, may be
censed individually, even if he [or she] is not the
officiant.) No distinction is to be made in the manner
of censing clergy and lay persons.[13]

There may be a second censing of the altar (but not of the officiant and people) at the *Magnificat.* This should be done at
least on Easter Day and on the eves of other feasts of our Lord,
with one or three circuits. This censing is also common on
Sunday and its eve.

On Easter Day and during its octave, and sometimes on
other occasions during the fifty days, Solemn Evensong takes
an ancient form known as Great Paschal Vespers. This liturgy
includes a procession down to the font and back to the rood
or chancel entrance.

If the officiant is a bishop . . . the devotions at the font
are led by a deacon, and those before the cross by a
priest. If the officiant is a priest, the prayers at the font
may be led by a lay reader [worship leader], and those
before the cross by a deacon.[14]

A deacon also sings a litany and the Easter dismissal with two
alleluias.

The Canadian church allows a deacon or other person to
preside at an evening service of light (as a single service or as
an introduction to Evensong). The leader sings or says an
opening acclamation and a solemn thanksgiving over the candle (BAS 61). This long blessing follows Jewish models.

5

# SEASONAL LITURGIES

EACH SEASON OF the church year has a special nature—its own face of Christ, its own relationship to incarnation and resurrection, its own readings, prayers, and songs, its own rites, its own smells and colors. The deacon helps to reinforce the season by wearing seasonal vestments and weaving seasonal themes into the intercessions. Seasonal litanies are available in a number of places, including online sources and four litanies of the Canadian church (see http://members.cox.net/oplater/prayer.htm and BAS 119–122).

## ADVENT

The deacon vests in an alb (or an alb resembling a dalmatic) and purple or blue stole, and may also wear a dalmatic in white or the same color as the stole.

## CHRISTMAS AND EPIPHANY

The deacon vests in an alb (or an alb resembling a dalmatic) and white or gold stole, and may also wear a dalmatic in white or gold.

In some places it is customary for a deacon (or someone else) to announce feasts and seasons. There are two main occasions for this custom. At Midnight Mass on Christmas, just before the entrance, a deacon may chant, "The Proclamation of Christmas." There is a similar proclamation on the Epiphany or the Baptism of our Lord, when a deacon may chant, "The Announcement of the Date of Easter" after the creed, or in place of it. On both occasions, accompanied by two candles, the deacon goes to the lectern (ambo) or other suitable place, and the people stand. Texts and music for these chants appear in the annual *Sourcebook for Sundays and Seasons,* published by Liturgy Training Publications in Chicago.

## CANDLEMAS

The deacon vests in an alb (or an alb resembling a dalmatic) and white or gold stole, and may also wear a dalmatic in white or gold. Immediately before the Eucharist, the congregation, after singing the *Nunc dimittis,* processes into church carrying lighted candles. To start the procession, the deacon directs, "Let us go forth in peace," and the people respond, "In the name of Christ. Amen" (BOS 54).[15]

## ASH WEDNESDAY

The deacon vests in an alb (or an alb resembling a dalmatic) and purple stole, and may also wear a dalmatic in white or purple.[16]

After the sermon, all standing, the deacon (or the presider) sings or says the invitation to a holy Lent. With others, the deacon may help the presider in the imposition of ashes (BCP 264–265; BAS 281–285). Using a thumb to mark the sign of the cross on the forehead, the deacon imposes ashes on the presider, and the presider on the deacon. It is helpful to dip the thumb in water or oil, or to mix them with the ashes, so that the ashes will adhere to thumb and forehead. Only the presider leads the litany of penitence, which substitutes for the prayers of the people. Two deacons attend a bishop who presides or is present.

In the absence of a bishop or priest, a deacon or licensed person presides at the entire Liturgy of the Word, including the rite of ashes. For the absolution at the end of the litany, the deacon "remains kneeling and substitutes the prayer for forgiveness appointed at Morning Prayer" (BCP 269; see BAS 286).

## LENT

The deacon vests in an alb (or an alb resembling a dalmatic) and purple stole, and may also wear a dalmatic in white or purple. When there are candidates for baptism, the deacon or other leader uses a special form of the prayers of the people on the first Sunday in Lent (BOS 124), unless the Great Litany is used. On all the Sundays in Lent, the deacon names the candidates and sponsors in the intercessions. In place of a blessing, the presider may sing or say a solemn prayer over the people, the deacon first directing, "Bow down before the Lord" (BOS 24).

## PALM SUNDAY

The deacon vests in an alb (or an alb resembling a dalmatic) and red stole, and may also wear a dalmatic in white or red.

In the Liturgy of the Palms, the deacon proclaims the gospel as usual: asks for and receives a blessing, announces the gospel, censes the book, sings or says the gospel, and gives the closing formula. To start the procession of palms, the deacon directs, "Let us go forth in peace," and the people respond, "In the name of Christ. Amen" (BCP 271; see BAS 299).

Two deacons attend a bishop who presides or is present.

In the absence of a bishop or priest, the Liturgy of the Palms may be led by a deacon or licensed lay person (BCP 272; BAS 299).

Chanting the passion gospel has a long history, dating from the fourth century in Jerusalem. In early times a deacon alone sang the gospel. The practice of using three singers became popular about the fourteenth century. Although the deacon or another soloist may chant the passion gospel, despite its length, it has become common for several other singers (not necessarily limited to three), and sometimes the whole congregation, to perform the passion. The prayer book allows the passion to be "read or chanted by lay persons" (BCP 273, 277; BAS 300). If three singers share the text, one takes the part of narrator, a second the part of Christ, and a third the other parts. The deacon usually takes the part of Christ or of narrator. All stand at the lectern, ambo, or pulpit. Several solo singers may take the roles of other persons in the narrative. The choir or congregation may perform the role of the crowd. Those who sing will need the music, or the congregation may sing on one note.

The readers recite the passion gospel with a special announcement ("The Passion of our Lord Jesus Christ, according to Matthew *or* Mark *or* Luke"), without salutation, without candles and censing, and without congregational responses before and after. At the account of the death of Christ, all kneel in silence (in old English usage, time enough to say a *Pater* and an *Ave,* or about thirty seconds). Then all rise for the closing section, which the narrator may sing solo to an elaborate old melody.[17]

## MAUNDY THURSDAY

The three days of Christ's death and resurrection, or Paschal Triduum (Latin for "three days"), follow the Jewish system of counting a day from sunset to sunset. The first day begins at sunset on Maundy Thursday, and the third day ends with sunset or Vespers on Easter Day. (For a discussion of the Chrism Mass, which is often held during the day on Maundy Thursday or earlier in Holy Week, see chapter 7.)

After sunset on Maundy Thursday, the cathedral and parish churches celebrate the beginning of the Triduum by recalling the Last Supper with a special Eucharist, known as the Mass of the Lord's Supper. Deacons function as usual. On this day and on all the three days, two deacons attend the bishop who presides. The deacon of the mass proclaims the gospel, leads or shares in leading the intercessions, and ministers at the altar. The deacon vests in an alb (or an alb resembling a dalmatic) and red stole (in some places white stole), and may also wear a dalmatic in white or red.

There are three distinctive ceremonies at the liturgy of Maundy Thursday:

*(1) Footwashing*
The ceremony of washing feet enacts the *mandatum novum,* or new commandment of love, in John 13:34. There is a long history of Christian footwashing, including the ancient baptismal rite in Milan, a medieval ceremony for welcoming guests at monasteries, and the liturgy of Maundy Thursday. In earlier centuries, on Maundy Thursday, those of high degree (kings, popes, bishops, abbots) washed the feet of those of low degree (peasants, seminarians, novices). In some congregations today, the priest washes the feet of parishioners, although this practice emphasizes outdated concepts of rank. More commonly, and in the spirit of our baptism, members of the congregation join in washing each other's feet.

The ceremony varies according to the customs of the congregation. Deacons may organize, oversee, and in some places perform the ceremony. They may change the introduction (BOS 93) to invite others to wash feet. In some places, the presider or organizer arranges for a few select people to have their feet washed. In other places, people informally come and go to a large tub or tubs in full view, sit to have their feet washed, and kneel to wash the feet of others. There must be piles of towels.

### (2) Reserving the sacrament

After the postcommunion prayer, the liturgy usually ends with reserving the sacrament for communion at the Good Friday liturgy. There are many ways of doing this. In one customary pattern, the presider puts on incense, kneels, and censes the sacrament remaining on the altar. Still kneeling, all sing "Now, my tongue, the mystery telling" (Hymn 329). Either during or after the hymn, the deacon or presider rises and takes the sacrament from the altar. Accompanied by candles, the deacon or presider carries it to a place apart from the main altar.

### (3) Stripping the altar

The deacon may help in stripping the altar, without ceremony. On Thursday and Friday during the sacred three days, the proper liturgy traditionally ends without a blessing (or prayer over the people) or dismissal. The liturgies of the Triduum are progressive acts in the paschal mystery of Christ. Intermissions of silence, fasting, and prayer separate the liturgies. With stops and starts, the sacred *anamnesis* or remembrance of our salvation goes on until finally it reaches a climax at the Easter Vigil.

## GOOD FRIDAY

The deacon vests in an alb (or an alb resembling a dalmatic) and red stole, and may also wear a dalmatic in white or red. Some Anglican clerics wear a black cassock (without surplice or stole) or black vestments.

The presider and deacon (and two acolytes) enter silently, reverence the altar, and kneel (or lie prostrate) before it, for at least a minute. Then they rise and go to their chairs. Singers or readers proclaim the passion gospel as on Palm Sunday. For the intercessions (titled in the prayer book "The Solemn Collects"), the deacon or another person, standing at the usual place, sings or says the introduction and biddings. The leader may adapt the "For" clauses by changing some, adding some, and omitting some. After each bidding the deacon may sing or say, "Let us kneel in silent prayer." After a significant period of silence (up to a minute), the same or another deacon commands, "Arise."

Then, if it is the custom, occurs the ceremony known as Veneration of the Cross (BCP 281; BAS 313). Worship before a cross has become familiar to Anglicans who attend Taizé liturgies, which often include a similar procession and veneration. The ceremony takes place simply or solemnly, in several ways. In one solemn form, suggesting the procession with the paschal candle at the Easter Vigil, the deacon goes to the entrance of the church and takes up a bare wooden cross. The cross may be large, requiring help to carry. Flanked by two acolytes bearing candles, the deacon enters the church and walks slowly toward the altar, pausing three times and (if possible) lifting the cross. Each time, the deacon sings at a higher pitch: "Behold the wood of the cross, on which hung the savior of the world." The people respond each time: "Come, let us worship." (BAS 313 gives two texts for this chant. The music may be found at http://members.cox.net/oplater/Eccelignum.pdf.) After each response, everyone else may kneel briefly in silence.

The deacon places the cross before the altar or in another convenient place in sight of the people, between the two candles. During the singing of anthems, perhaps including a form of the Reproaches (see texts in BAS 314–317), the people remain in their seats in meditation or come forward to kneel or bow before the cross and often to kiss or touch it. The hymn "Sing, my tongue, the glorious battle" (Hymn 165 or 166) concludes the veneration.

"In the absence of a bishop or priest, all that precedes may be led by a deacon or lay reader [worship leader]" (BCP 282). In this liturgy, as in others, a deacon presides only when the normal presider is absent.

Normally (if not always), communion from the reserved sacrament follows. After the hymn "Sing, my tongue, the glorious battle,"[18] the deacon rises and spreads the corporal on the bare altar. The deacon carries the reserved sacrament to the altar and places it on the cloth, all in silence. Two acolytes with candles accompany the deacon and place the candles on or near the altar. The presider comes to the altar for the confession of sin and the Lord's Prayer. After communion, the deacon and others consume the remaining sacrament (unless there is to be another liturgy with communion that day), clear the altar, and cleanse the vessels. After the final prayers, all go in silence, without blessing or dismissal.

## HOLY SATURDAY

The time between cross and resurrection calls for silence, not sounds and ceremonies. If there is to be the proper Liturgy of the Word on Holy Saturday, however, it appropriately takes the place of the noonday office. After the entrance, there may be a period of silence, which according to Howard Galley may be led in the following manner:

> Facing the people, the celebrant chants: "Let us pray."
> The deacon (or celebrant) then sings "Let us kneel in silent prayer." At the conclusion of the silence the deacon chants "Arise." All then stand; and the celebrant chants the Collect of the Day.[19]

The deacon announces the gospel, "The Conclusion of the Passion of our Lord Jesus Christ according to Matthew *or* John." The people omit the usual responses.

## THE GREAT VIGIL OF EASTER

The supreme feast of the Christian year calls for the active participation of all ordained ministers, each in their order, and all other baptized persons. "It is the prerogative of a deacon to carry the Paschal Candle to its place, and to chant the Exsultet. Deacons likewise assist at Baptism and the Eucharist according to their order" (BCP 284; BAS 321).[20] The deacon vests in an alb (or an alb resembling a dalmatic) and white or gold stole, and may also wear a dalmatic in white or gold.

Normally, the vigil begins in darkness outside the church or, in foul weather, inside the church or a nearby hall. Fire is kindled, and the presider addresses the people and says a prayer. In some places, the presider cuts a cross in the candle, traces the Greek letters A (alpha) and Ω (omega) and the numbers of the year, and inserts five grains of incense in the wax (see the rites in BAS 333). The presider or the deacon lights the paschal candle from the new fire.

Carrying the candle, the deacon leads the people into the darkened church, pausing three times, lifting the candle, and singing the chant (found in the Hymnal at S 68), each time at a higher pitch: "The light of Christ." The people respond: "Thanks be to God." (Note the resemblance to the entrance of the cross on Good Friday.) Preferably the deacon pauses at the start, the church door, and the chancel. If the people gather indoors, the pauses take place at the door, halfway through the nave, and before the altar.

At the start, or before placing the candle in its stand near the lectern or pulpit, the deacon gives those nearby a chance to light their handheld candles from the paschal candle. In some places, the people light their candles before entering church; in others, they enter in near darkness. The light spreads through the congregation, candle to candle.

The deacon puts the candle in its stand, goes to the presider (who has meanwhile come to the chair), and helps in putting incense on the coals. The deacon bows deeply before the presider and asks: "Father *or* Mother, give me your blessing."

The presider replies with a variation of the blessing before the gospel: "The Lord be in your heart and on your lips, that you may worthily proclaim his paschal praise: In the name of the Father, and of the Son, and of the Holy Spirit." The deacon replies: "Amen."

The deacon returns to the candle, takes the censer, and censes the candle by walking around it counterclockwise (if possible). Facing the people across the candle, or nearby, the deacon sings the Exsultet. The deacon uses the Altar Book or other musical text at the lectern or pulpit, or in the dimness sings from memory. The lack of light during the Exsultet is frequently a problem for the deacon, and others may have to stand close by with candles or small flashlights to illuminate the book. In the introductory "Rejoice" stanzas, sung to the people, the deacon keeps hands joined; from the salutation on, in the long prayer addressed to the Father, the deacon extends hands in the *orans* or prayer gesture.

In some congregations, the deacon changes the text in several places. Usually, "fathers" becomes "forebears" or "ancestors," and "man" becomes "humankind" or "human beings." It is also common to add two traditional passages omitted in the prayer book version: (1) at the end of the first "How" stanza, "O happy fault, O necessary sin of Adam, which gained for us so great a redeemer," and (2) at the end of the phrase about the candle, "the work of the bees your creatures." Such changes and additions are not permitted by the rubrics, and they should be used only with the permission of the presider or bishop. The Anglican Church of Canada allows use of a different translation and musical setting (BAS 334). The music is not canonically regulated, however, and several chants are available online, including the music of the Roman rite (the one in the Altar Book), the Ambrosian preface tone, and the ancient Beneventan chant of southern Italy. (For links to Exsultet chant pages, see http://members.cox.net/oplater/index.htm.)

The Exsultet may include a visual display, recalling the large illustrations on the Exsultet scrolls of southern Italy in the Middle Ages. As the deacon sang the Exsultet, he gradually unrolled the scroll over the front of the ambo, and the pictures became visible to those standing around.[21] Similarly, during Lent the children of the congregation may prepare pictures of scenes such as Adam and Eve, crossing the Red Sea, and the resurrection of Christ, to be revealed as the deacon sings about those events.

The deacon helps at baptism, proclaims the gospel, and ministers at the table (see chapters 2 and 3). The prayer book requires the prayers of the people at the Easter Vigil, even when there has been a baptism. This is an occasion when a newly composed text of the prayers is appropriate. The deacon sings or says the Easter dismissal with "alleluia, alleluia," here and throughout the fifty days.

> In the absence of a bishop or priest, a deacon or lay reader [worship leader] may lead the first two parts of the service, the Renewal of Baptismal Vows, and the Ministry of the Word of the Vigil Eucharist, concluding with the Prayers of the People, the Lord's Prayer, and the Dismissal. A deacon may also, when the services of a priest cannot be obtained, and with the authorization of the bishop, officiate at public Baptism; and may administer Easter Communion

from the Sacrament previously consecrated. (BCP 284; see BAS 321)

## THE DAY OF PENTECOST

If a vigil is held on Saturday night, the deacon functions as usual in the service of light, helping with incense. The paschal candle is already lit. The deacon vests in an alb (or an alb resembling a dalmatic) and white or red stole, and may also wear a dalmatic in white or red.

In many places, at some or all the liturgies of Pentecost, several persons read the gospel or the reading from Acts 2 in ancient and foreign languages. All gather at the ambo or other place of reading. If the reading is the gospel, the deacon announces the gospel in English (or other language of the congregation) and censes the book. Starting with the oldest language, the others then read the gospel, without announcement or closing. Finally, the deacon reads the gospel in the local language and gives the closing formula.

6

# PASTORAL LITURGIES

## REAFFIRMATION OF BAPTISMAL VOWS

*The Book of Occasional Services 2003* provides four stages of reaffirmation of baptismal vows (BOS 136–145). These are parallel to the stages of the catechumenate (described in chapter 2 of this book) but are for those who have already been baptized, including penitents. The traditional role of deacons suggests that they function in two main ways:

(1) Deacons make sure that those preparing for reaffirmation become involved in works of mercy and justice.

(2) Deacons include the names of those preparing for reaffirmation in the prayers of the people.

The liturgies of reaffirmation mention deacons only once. In the first stage, at the welcoming of baptized persons into the community, a deacon or sponsor calls out their names as they are written in the church register (BOS 141).

## CONFIRMATION

If enough deacons are available, two attend the bishop, and a third proclaims the gospel reading, may lead the intercessions (if used), and ministers at the altar (see chapter 3 and appendix).

The prayer book allows the use of the prayers for the baptismal candidates (BCP 417, but BAS 627 requires a different litany). Because some of the petitions are redundant for those already baptized, it is better to omit or replace them. Howard Galley provides a model form of the prayers of the people at baptism and confirmation in *Ceremonies of the Eucharist* (pp. 231–232). Paul V. Marshall suggests that the prayers for the candidates on Sunday "may well be followed without pause by intercessions and thanksgivings appropriate to the place and time."[22]

## A FORM OF COMMITMENT TO CHRISTIAN SERVICE

The rite comes before the preparation of the table (BCP 420). To the preceding prayers of the people, the deacon may add the name of the person making or renewing a covenant.

## THE CELEBRATION AND BLESSING
## OF A MARRIAGE

In addition to reading the gospel and otherwise helping at the Eucharist (if celebrated), the deacon may deliver the charge and ask for the declaration of consent (both at BCP 424). The Canadian church reserves these two functions to the presider (BAS 529). "The Deacon or other person appointed" leads the nuptial prayers of the people (BCP 429–430; BAS 533).

"Where it is permitted by civil law that deacons may perform marriages, and no priest or bishop is available, a deacon may use the service which follows [the marriage rite], omitting the nuptial blessing which follows The Prayers" (BCP 422; see BAS 527). A similar rubric applies to the Order for Marriage (BCP 435). In many dioceses, a deacon presides at a marriage only with the specific authorization of the bishop; some bishops restrict such presidency to priests.

## THE BLESSING OF A CIVIL MARRIAGE

This liturgy is for couples who have already been married in a civil ceremony. The blessing takes places within the Eucharist, after the homily. For the prayers of the people, the deacon or other leader uses the nuptial prayers (BCP 434; prayers on BCP 428).

## AN ORDER FOR MARRIAGE

This order allows the bride and groom to make choices other than those provided in the prayer book. The deacon helps as in the normal marriage rite and may preside only under certain restrictions (see above). The order permits the composition of intercessions "for the husband and wife, for their life together, for the Christian community, and for the world" (BCP 436).

## A THANKSGIVING FOR THE BIRTH
## OR ADOPTION OF A CHILD

The ceremony takes place within the Eucharist, following the prayers of the people. The deacon or other leader of intercession may mention the names of the child and parents (BCP 439).

## THE RECONCILIATION OF A PENITENT

Each of the two forms for sacramental confession provides a "Declaration of Forgiveness to be used by a Deacon or Lay Person":

Our Lord Jesus Christ, who offered himself to be sacrificed for us to the Father, forgives your sins by the grace of the Holy Spirit. (BCP 448, 452; BAS 169, 171)

The penitent replies "Amen." A deacon uses the provision mainly in an emergency such as impending death or isolated imprisonment, when a bishop or priest is unobtainable. Nevertheless, when pastoral prudence and charity lead a deacon to hear a confession, the deacon should first state clearly that the confessor will declare forgiveness but not pronounce absolution.

"The secrecy of a confession is morally absolute for the confessor, and must under no circumstances be broken" (BCP 446; BAS 166). This requirement of strict confidentiality applies equally to all who hear a confession, including deacons, whether or not they pronounce absolution.

If, for sound reason, sacramental confession, or at least absolution, takes place in the presence of a congregation, the deacon functions as usual in the preceding Liturgy of the Word and the following Liturgy of the Sacrament. The true goal, and climax, of reconciliation is rejoining in communion with God and others.

## MINISTRATION TO THE SICK

Bishops and priests provide the main sacramental and pastoral care for the sick. From early times, however, deacons and other baptized persons have visited and cared for the sick, as Christ teaches in Matthew 25:31–46. Ideally, the church in all her orders and ministries comes to the bedside for prayer, anointing, and communion. As a practical reality, the visitor, whether bishop, priest, deacon, or any other baptized person, often vis-

its alone and thus functions visibly as a sign of the church beyond the sickroom.

Today, deacons often visit the sick in close cooperation with
priests and others. They also organize, train, and lead teams of
baptized ministers. In such an arrangement, a deacon may
function as liturgical leader, whose pastoral visit culminates in
a rite of word and sacrament.

There are three settings for rites for the sick: private, small
group, and public. These rites are located in three books:

*(1) The Book of Common Prayer*
The rites for visiting the sick are designed for private or public settings. In practice they are used mainly for private visitations.

Ministration to the Sick (BCP 453–457) consists of three
sections—Ministry of the Word, Laying on of Hands and
Anointing, and Holy Communion—used separately or
(preferably) together. A deacon or other visitor chooses among
four sets of readings—each with epistle, psalm, and gospel—
or any other passage of scripture. The visitor needs to use only
part of a set. A few verses (such as the angel passage in Psalm
91) provide material for comment on the Christian meaning
of sickness and death. The visitor may then offer prayers (several are given in BCP 458–460) or a litany, mentioning the
sick person by name. The visitor may help the sick person
make a general confession. (For the restricted use of sacramental confession, see above.)

Bishops and parish priests (the "elders" of James 5:14) lay
hands on and anoint the sick. Ancient custom, common sense,
and the prayer book give the ministry also to deacons and

other baptized persons. "In cases of necessity, a deacon or lay person may perform the anointing, using oil blessed by a bishop or priest" (BCP 456; see BAS 555). Since necessity occurs whenever a person is seriously ill or preparing for surgery and no bishop or priest is available, Episcopal and other Anglican deacons should seize the opportunity to offer this outward and visible sign of Christian health. (The Roman Catholic Church restricts anointing to bishops and priests.)

Oil of the sick (*oleo infirmorum*), sometimes soaked in a wad of cotton, is usually carried in a small bottle or metal vessel (known as an oil stock). The deacon dips a thumb in the oil and marks a cross on the sick person's forehead, saying the anointing sentence. It is sometimes desirable to anoint another place on the body—lips, throat, hands, or other site of disease. The deacon may point out that the sign of the cross on the forehead recalls the signing in baptism, and that we receive true healing through union with Christ and his church. In ancient times, Christians used copious amounts of pure olive oil, and sick persons sometimes drank it like a tonic.

Although the prayer book appears to reserve the laying on of hands to priests, it allows deacons and others to use anointing. The term "anointing" stands for the entire rite, as does "unction" in the Catechism (BCP 861). The Canadian church allows deacons and lay persons authorized by the diocesan bishop to anoint with oil (BAS 555). The rite in *Enriching Our Worship 2* permits any baptized person to lay on hands and anoint (see below). In conclusion, deacons may use both hands and oil in public and private rites of healing.

After the anointing, the deacon opens the pyx or other container of bread (and the bottle or cruet of wine, if any) and begins the communion rite with the Lord's Prayer, first saying: "Let us pray in the words our Savior Christ has taught us." The deacon gives communion with the usual words. If the person is near death, the deacon may use "other words" (see BCP 399). From ancient times, Christians have referred to the final communion of a dying person as *viaticum* (provisions for a journey). The deacon may give communion with these or similar words: "*N.*, receive this food for your journey, the body of Christ, the bread of heaven." For the wine, the deacon adds: "The blood of Christ, the cup of salvation." If the bread and wine are received together by intinction, the deacon combines the words.

If the sick person is unable to receive the sacrament, the deacon "is to assure that person that all the benefits of Communion are received, even though the Sacrament is not received with the mouth" (BCP 457). Then the deacon holds the bread (and wine) before the person and says the words of administration. Others in the sickroom may receive by mouth. Communion ends with a prayer and "Let us bless the Lord."

If a stole is worn, even over street clothes, the deacon wears it hanging from the left shoulder in the manner of a deacon.

*(2) The Book of Occasional Services*

The liturgy titled A Public Service of Healing (BOS 166–173) is designed for a congregation. If the rite takes place within the Eucharist, as is preferable, the deacon functions as usual. A litany of healing, led by a person appointed, may replace the prayers of the people. It is not clear whether anyone other than the presiding priest may anoint. Perhaps unintentionally, the following rubric fails to mention deacons (and other priests who are present): "Lay persons with a gift of healing may join the celebrant in the laying on of hands" (BOS 170). Without an explicit prohibition, deacons and other priests may lay on hands and anoint.

### (3) Enriching Our Worship 2

Under the title *Ministry with the Sick or Dying* (Church Publishing, 2000), *Enriching Our Worship 2* provides a full and flexible set of liturgies, including services in churches, homes, hospitals, nursing homes, and other healthcare facilities. The emphasis is on public liturgies, starting with A Public Service of Healing (EOW2 27–45). Ministry in a Home or Health Care Facility (EOW2 46–58) will usually be either private or for a small group. Distribution of Holy Communion by eucharistic visitors (EOW2 59–63) is normally for private or small group use.

The rubrics and structure of these liturgies are similar to Ministration to the Sick in the prayer book. The rubric governing ministers gives broad permission for deacons and other baptized persons, in the absence of a bishop or priest, to lead services, lay on hands and anoint the sick, and give communion (EOW2 24–25). In the rite itself, a rubric says that laying on of hands and anointing "may be administered by a lay or ordained minister" (EOW2 52).

## MINISTRATION AT THE TIME OF DEATH

If a person is near death, the deacon should give communion immediately, followed by the prayers at the time of death (BCP

462–465; see BAS 560–564). If there is time, the deacon may use these prayers within the three parts of the Ministration to the Sick:

*(1) At the end of the Liturgy of the Word:* the prayer "Almighty God, look on this your servant" and the Litany at the Time of Death (BCP 462; BAS 562);

*(2) Just before communion:* the Lord's Prayer and collect "Deliver your servant" (BCP 464; BAS 562);

*(3) In place of the postcommunion prayer and dismissal:* one or more of the prayers "Depart, O Christian soul," "Into your hands," and "May *his* soul" (BCP 464–465; see BAS 563–564).

*Enriching Our Worship 2* (pp. 96–127) provides additional litanies, prayers, and forms for laying on hands, anointing, and administering communion from the reserved sacrament. There are also prayers for discontinuing life-support.

## THE BURIAL OF THE DEAD

Prayer book rites for the Burial of the Dead consist of a series of liturgies or stations during a journey. At each station, the community of Christians gathers around the body or ashes of the dead person for prayer and remembrance. The journey begins before death with liturgies of sickness and dying. The prayer book anticipates that the following will be the normal practice.

After death, on the night before burial or just before the funeral, a vigil (or wake) takes place at the home of the dead person, in church, or elsewhere. The deacon or other leader uses the Litany at the Time of Death or the litany provided for a vigil (BCP 462, 465; EOW3 13; see BAS 571–575); the people may need a copy of these prayers. Either litany may take place within Evening Prayer, said or sung or celebrated solemnly. If incense is used at the candle-lighting, the deacon also censes the body or ashes, usually by walking around the coffin or container. The proper for Evensong of the dead includes: Psalm 116 (antiphon: "I will walk in the presence of the Lord in the land of the living"); Psalm 121 (antiphon: "The Lord shall preserve you from all evil; it is he who shall keep you safe"); John 14:1–6; and the *Magnificat* (antiphon: "Everyone the Father gives to me will come to me; I will never turn away anyone who believes in me"). Alternatively, a Vigil of the Resurrection may be sung, perhaps throughout the night (see EOW3 15–17).

Reception of the body or ashes takes place on the arrival at church. The deacon or other person (such as a family member) leads the procession bearing the lighted paschal candle. When the coffin or container, covered with a pall or other cloth, reaches a resting place before the altar, the deacon places the candle in its stand nearby. The deacon may also place the book of gospels on the coffin or container or nearby, open to the passage to be read at the funeral.

In the burial Eucharist, the deacon functions as usual. The deacon proclaims the gospel, perhaps reading from the book on the coffin or container. The deacon or other leader sings or says the prayers of the people, using one of the three forms

(BCP 465, 480, 497; but see BAS 579, 593). The Rite Two form is suitable if the gospel reading has been John 11:21–27 ("I am the resurrection and the life"). *Enriching Our Worship 3* provides four additional forms (EOW3 79–83). It is often desirable to include several family members and friends in leading the prayers. If incense is used at the preparation of the table, the deacon (or presider) may conclude by walking around the body or ashes.

The Eucharist ends with the commendation, at which the presider, deacon, and other ministers come to stand near the body. During the singing of the *kontakion* ("Give rest, O Christ"), if the presider sprinkles the body or ashes with water or uses incense, the deacon helps in the usual way. The deacon dismisses the people with "Let us go forth in the name of Christ." Although the rite doesn't provide the Easter form of dismissal, the deacon should add two alleluias during the fifty days and maybe, since burial is "an Easter liturgy" (BCP 507), at any other time.

"When the services of a priest cannot be obtained, a deacon or lay reader [worship leader] may preside at the service," omitting the Liturgy of the Sacrament (BCP 468, 490; see BAS 571).

In the committal at the grave (or scattering of ashes), the deacon may take parts not assigned to the presider. The deacon may locate some real dirt and distribute it for casting on the coffin or container of ashes.

*Enriching Our Worship 3,* under the title *Burial Rites for Adults together with a Rite for the Burial of a Child* (Church Publishing, 2007), provides liturgies similar to those in the prayer book, but greatly expanded and enriched. In the Eucharist the deacon functions as usual. Strangely, there are still no alleluias with the Easter dismissal.

## THE BURIAL OF A DEACON

The funeral of a deacon, like others in holy orders, calls for special ceremonies recognizing the deacon's role in the church. The following may be used intact or adapted.

The body of the deacon is dressed in Easter vestments and placed in a simple coffin, or the ashes are placed in a simple container. As soon as possible, the coffin or container is brought to the cathedral or to the parish church where the deacon served. The bishop, with deacons, receives the body or ashes at the church door, and escorts the body or ashes to a place before the altar. Deacons may carry the coffin or container and place it on the floor in front of the altar. A dalmatic, stole, and other appropriate symbols are placed on the coffin or nearby.

At the vigil, the bishop, attended by two deacons and with other deacons as choir, celebrates Solemn Evensong. In the absence of the bishop, a priest or senior deacon officiates at the reception and vigil. Deacons and others close to the life and ministry of the dead deacon help with the liturgies.

At the burial Eucharist, two deacons attend the presider (preferably the bishop). When a bishop presides, three deacons serve as usual (see chapter 7). Other deacons gather in the chancel or nearby and form a choir for the liturgy. Priests of the diocese may concelebrate, space permitting. Family members bake the bread and present the bread and wine. Incense is always appropriate for a deacon.

At the commendation, the presider and all the deacons gather near the body or ashes. Deacons carry the coffin or container out of church or escort the body or ashes. If possible, they complete the burial by taking part in the committal at the grave or in the scattering of ashes.

## AN ORDER FOR BURIAL

This order (BCP 506) allows the family and friends to make choices other than those provided in the prayer book. If the rite includes the Eucharist, the deacon helps as in normal burial.

## OTHER PASTORAL LITURGIES

*The Book of Occasional Services 2003* provides liturgies for numerous other pastoral occasions. Those including a deacon, at least implicitly, are the following.

### WELCOMING NEW PEOPLE TO A CONGREGATION (BOS 112)

The deacon or other leader may mention the names of new members in the prayers of the people. Then, just before the peace, they are introduced to the congregation.

### WHEN MEMBERS LEAVE A CONGREGATION (BOS 113)

On their last Sunday, the deacon or other leader may mention the departure of these members before the prayers of the people and then add their names to the prayers.

CELEBRATION FOR A HOME (BOS 146–156)
The prayers during the procession through the house take the place of the prayers of the people. The blessing of the house appropriately takes place within the Eucharist, in which the deacon functions as usual. (*The Book of Occasional Services 2003* also provides home blessings for Epiphany and Easter, without the Eucharist, 47–50, 99–102.)

THE PREPARATION OF PARENTS AND GODPARENTS FOR THE BAPTISM OF INFANTS AND YOUNG CHILDREN (BOS 159–162)
This process involves three stages:

> (1) The blessing of the prospective parents (or pregnant mother), preferably within the Eucharist, after the prayers of the people (BOS 157–158).
>
> (2) Thanksgiving for the birth or adoption of a child (BCP 439–445).
>
> (3) Baptism (BCP 299–308).

ANNIVERSARY OF A MARRIAGE (BOS 163–165)
The liturgy takes place within the Eucharist. At a principal service, the deacon or other leader may add the names of the husband and wife to the prayers of the people.

A PUBLIC SERVICE OF HEALING (BOS 166–173)
See above, Ministration to the Sick.

## CONCERNING EXORCISM (BOS 174)

In the early church exorcisms "were reserved to the bishop, at whose discretion they might be delegated to selected presbyters and others deemed competent." Today the bishop alone may designate who performs the rite.

## BURIAL OF ONE WHO DOES NOT PROFESS THE CHRISTIAN FAITH (BOS 175–178)

The deacon functions mainly by proclaiming the only gospel reading provided, John 10:11–16.

## COMMISSIONING FOR LAY MINISTRIES IN THE CHURCH (BOS 179–195)

A deacon who has a pastoral connection with the ministers, such as leading or training them in ministry, may act as sponsor in presenting them for commissioning. The deacon may mention them in the prayers of the people.

## DEDICATION OF CHURCH FURNISHINGS AND ORNAMENTS (BOS 196–213)

Deacons accompany and help the presider, especially when the bishop dedicates an altar, a font, chalices and patens, and a bell. At the end of the dedication, "the benefactors and persons to be commemorated may be remembered in the Prayers of the People" (BOS 212).

## THE FOUNDING OF A CHURCH (BOS 214–220)

During the procession to the site where ground is to be broken, a deacon or other person sings or says the litany for the church (provided in the rite). At the end, the deacon dismisses the people.

## LITURGIES FOR CHURCH PLANTING (BOS 223–314)
This series of liturgies is given in three languages: English, Spanish, and French. Deacons function as usual in the Eucharist, but with a couple of exceptions. There appears to be a change from the prayer book practice of dismissing with "alleluia, alleluia" only in the Easter season, instead permitting alleluias to be used any time except in Lent. The rubric states: "In Lent, the alleluias are omitted. In the Easter Season, they are included." Another rubric names the minister of the dismissal in a eucharistic liturgy as "Officiant/Celebrant" instead of the usual "Deacon or Celebrant" (BOS 243, 273, 305).

## RESTORING OF THINGS PROFANED (BOS 317–318)
Deacons may help with blessed water or incense, often used as signs of purification.

## SECULARIZING A CONSECRATED BUILDING (BOS 319–321)
If the bishop presides, deacons help as usual.

## GUIDELINES FOR USE ON THE OCCASION OF A RETIREMENT OR WORK TRANSITION (BOS 327–328)
The celebration normally occurs within the Eucharist, in which the deacon serves as usual. "Family members or friends might read the Prayers of the People, which could be adapted to the occasion" (BOS 327).

7

# LITURGIES WITH
# A BISHOP

THE BISHOP IS CALLED and ordained to "exercise without reproach the high priesthood" (BCP 521). This priestly role includes offering the holy gifts and overseeing the life and work of the diocese. When present at liturgy, therefore, the bishop presides and preaches whenever possible. Even when the bishop is absent, the assembly gathers around the presidency of the bishop, delegated to a priest or presbyter.

Some liturgies require a bishop. In diocesan liturgies, especially, the people of God assemble as the body of Christ. Called together by God, they gather in a rich and diverse array—bishop presiding, presbyters in collegial leadership, deacons in communal service, all God's people in priestly worship. All unite themselves with the mystery and joy of the risen Christ. All hear the good news of salvation, offer intercession and thanksgiving, and receive the food of eternal life. All give glory to God the Father, through Jesus Christ our Lord, in the unity of the Holy Spirit, and God gives all the gift of Christ, present in holy people, holy word, and holy things. Empowered by the Spirit, all go forth to pursue God's mission in the world.

The ordination rites present the church with an opportunity to show the three orders, surrounded by all the ministers and people, as distinct ministers with special responsibilities, special relationships, and special significance. The three orders are "a gift from God for the nurture of his people and the proclamation of his Gospel everywhere" (BCP 510; BAS 631). As Ignatius of Antioch says: "Just as where Jesus Christ is, the catholic church is, where the bishop is, all the people should be" (*Ad Smyrnaeos,* 8, 2). And where the bishop and all the people are, the presbyters and deacons should be.

## EUCHARIST WITH A BISHOP

When a bishop presides in the Eucharist, deacons serve in numbers depending on the size and character of the celebration.

### One deacon
A single deacon functions as usual in the Eucharist and, preferably with other ministers, assists the bishop with mitre, pastoral staff (crozier), and books.

### Two deacons
Both deacons assist the bishop, one on each side at the chair and at the altar. The right deacon also acts as deacon of the mass, proclaiming the gospel and assisting at the altar and with

elevating the cup. The left deacon helps with mitre, staff, and books, and turns pages at the altar. Both may assist in giving communion. Bearing the gospel book, the right deacon walks ahead of concelebrants and the bishop. The left deacon walks a little behind the bishop and to the right. Another minister, helping with the staff, may walk to the left.

### Three deacons

Especially at major celebrations with a bishop, three deacons serve. One takes the role of deacon of the mass. The other two serve as attending deacons, sometimes called bishop's chaplains.

The deacon of the mass bears the gospel book, enters ahead of the other deacons, concelebrating priests and bishops, and the bishop with attending deacons, and places the book on the altar. The deacon proclaims the gospel reading, leads the intercessions (or shares in them) and the confession of sin, censes the bishop and people, assists at the altar and with elevating the cup, may assist in giving communion, cleans up, perhaps makes announcements, and gives the dismissal (immediately after the bishop's blessing).

The attending deacons assist the bishop, one on each side, helping with mitre, crozier, and books. Before the liturgy, they vest first and help the bishop to vest. At the entrance, they walk a little behind the bishop. After receiving the mitre and staff, they reverence the altar with the bishop. During the Liturgy of the Word, the left deacon helps with staff and Altar Book, and the right deacon handles the mitre. The bishop wears the mitre while seated for the readings and (without mitre) holds the staff during the gospel. At censings of the altar, both deacons may go with the bishop, the right before and the left after, or they may stand aside. If the bishop wears a zucchetto or purple skull cap, one of the deacons removes it just before the eucharistic prayer and returns it when the bishop arrives back at the chair after giving communion. During the eucharistic prayer, both deacons stand behind the bishop (if possible) or aside. Both deacons may assist the bishop in giving communion, at the rail or at a station. After communion, they return to the chair with the bishop. On leaving, they reverence the altar with the bishop and follow the bishop out.

In large liturgies it may be convenient to have two lay ministers, vested in alb or surplice, to assist the attending deacons. They walk in procession behind the attending deacons and handle the mitre and staff when those items are not in use.

### Other deacons

Another deacon, vested with dalmatic and stole or simply in cassock and surplice, may function as master of ceremonies and help at the altar by turning pages. Other deacons may give communion.

On occasion, a bishop functions liturgically (for example, as preacher) without presiding. If possible, one or two deacons attend the bishop, remaining nearby.

## THE ORDINATION OF A BISHOP

"Representatives of the presbyterate, diaconate, and laity of the diocese for which the new bishop is to be consecrated, are assigned appropriate duties in the service" (BCP 511; BAS 632).

Although the rubrics allow a deacon or a priest (but not a bishop) to proclaim the gospel, normally a deacon does this. Deacons prepare the table and gifts, and a deacon dismisses the people.

Although it is possible to ordain a bishop with only one deacon, several are desirable. As many as five deacons may serve as major assistants. Two attend the chief consecrator throughout the rite, handling mitre, staff, and books. After the ordination prayer, two other deacons attend the new bishop, helping in vesting and in giving symbols. Where it is the custom, during the hymn *Veni Creator Spiritus* the same two may hold the book of the gospels open and face down over the head of the kneeling bishop-elect. (Although in the Roman rite this ceremony takes place during the ordination prayer, in Anglican usage it interferes with the laying on of hands at that point.) The deacon of the mass serves as usual by proclaiming the gospel and ministering at the altar (see chapter 3). Other deacons, if present, give communion and help with cleansing the vessels. (See the appendix for detailed functions of deacons in the Ordination of a Bishop.)

## THE ORDINATION OF A PRIEST

The rubrics provide for the ordination of one or several priests. Today, in most dioceses, there will usually be sufficient deacons to serve in the liturgy.

A deacon or a priest (if deacons are absent) proclaims the gospel and dismisses the people, and deacons prepare the table. (Curiously, the prayer book provides for the absence of a deacon at the gospel and dismissal but requires deacons at the preparation of the table [BCP 529 and 535]. The Canadian church requires a deacon only for the dismissal [BAS 650].) Preferably two deacons attend the ordaining bishop. The deacon of the mass serves as usual by proclaiming the gospel and ministering at the altar (see chapter 3). This deacon may also assist the bishop with the gifts symbolizing the ministry of priesthood: Bible, paten with bread, and chalice with wine (the bread and wine to be offered at the altar). Vesting the new priest is usually handled by priests of the diocese. Other deacons, if present, give communion.

The new priest joins the bishop at the altar for the eucharistic prayer and fraction. When a deacon ministers on the right, the priest stands on the left side of the bishop. (See the appendix for detailed functions of deacons in the Ordination of a Priest.)

## THE ORDINATION OF DEACONS

When the ordination rites of the Episcopal Church were drafted in the late 1960s, they assumed the ordination of only one deacon at a time but provided for several. The Canadian ordination rites drafted in the early 1980s made similar assumptions and provisions. Now it is common for bishops to ordain deacons in groups.

Deacons chosen for the diaconate normally are ordained separately from deacons chosen ultimately for the priesthood, although joint ordinations are the practice in a few dioceses. In some dioceses, the bishop uses a single liturgy to ordain deacons and priests (and sometimes to commission other ministers in a parish).

The presence of other deacons supports those joining their company. Preferably two deacons attend the bishop, and the deacon of the mass proclaims the gospel reading. Other deacons walk in procession ahead of the bishop and may give communion. Although deacons do not join in the laying on of hands (as bishops and priests do in ordinations of their sacramental colleagues), they may stand behind or near the bishop during the ordination prayer. Their company symbolizes a ministerial relationship among themselves and with their bishop. The active participation of each ordinand's spouse and children, if any, and others who serve in Christ emphasizes *diakonia* as a vital function of the Christian community.

The ordination takes place either in the cathedral or in some other church or place large enough to accommodate a sizeable assembly, on a Sunday, feast day, or other day when many persons can attend. The ordinands wear surplices or preferably albs, without other vesture or adornment. Dalmatics and stoles may be laid out near the altar or carried in the entrance procession (usually by presenters). The ordinands and their presenters walk ahead of the deacon carrying the book of the gospels. "A Priest and a Lay Person, and additional presenters if desired" (BCP 538; BAS 653), who may include deacons, present each ordinand to the bishop, either together or in succession.

Someone sings the Litany for Ordinations "or some other approved litany" (BCP 539). The litany of saints, adapted for deacons, may be used for this purpose. The Canadian church provides a choice of two litanies, to be sung after the exami-

nation (BAS 656). During the litany, the ordinands kneel
(with everyone else) or lie prostrate. (According to ancient custom, if the ordination takes place during the fifty days of Easter
or on Sundays, all others may remain standing.) The deacons
of the diocese, each holding a lit candle, may join the gospel
procession, perhaps going around the side aisles to return up
the center. Drawing from the scriptural readings, the bishop
normally preaches on the meaning and duties of the diaconate;
the bishop may appoint someone else, including a deacon, to
preach.

For the examination, the ordinands, unattended and preferably without a book or program, come and stand before the
bishop. All should have memorized their responses.

After the examination, the ordinands kneel before the
bishop, on pillows provided for that purpose. The people sing
one of two designated hymns to the Spirit (usually *Veni Creator Spiritus*). A period of silent prayer follows. The bishop
then sings or says the ordination prayer with hands out-
stretched. At the epiclesis, the bishop goes to each ordinand
in turn (or each one comes to the bishop and kneels in turn)
and lays hands on the ordinand's head, saying:

> Therefore, Father, through Jesus Christ your Son, give
> your Holy Spirit to *N;* fill *him* with grace and power
> and make *him* a deacon in your Church." (BCP 545;
> see BAS 657)

The bishop finishes the prayer, all respond with a loud
"Amen," and the new deacons rise.

Other deacons, spouses, or others vest the new deacons in
stole and dalmatic. This is often a time of uncertainty and fum-

bling, especially if the stoles are the long Byzantine kind. Then the new deacons approach the bishop again, in turn, and kneel to receive a Bible. This is usually an individual Bible with the deacon's name engraved on it; instead, the bishop may present the lectionary Bible to each new deacon. Following an old custom, the bishop may also present the book of the gospels to each new deacon, still kneeling, saying:

Receive the gospel of Christ, whose herald you are.
Believe what you receive, teach what you believe, and
do what you teach.

The deacon kisses the book and hands it to an attending deacon or other minister.[23]

At the peace, the new deacons may exchange an embrace first with the bishop, then with nearby priests and deacons, then with spouse, children, and others. As a first liturgical act, a new deacon may direct all present to exchange the kiss: "Offer one another a sign of peace."

From then on, the new deacons serve in the eucharistic liturgy (replacing the deacons who served up to that point). All stand behind or near the altar. Two attend the bishop. One or two prepare the table. One censes the bishop and people. One serves at the bishop's right side, lifting the cup. Some give communion. Some consume the remaining elements and cleanse the vessels. Right after the bishop's blessing, one sings or says the dismissal, or all sing it in unison. All accompany the bishop out of the church. All may carry the sacrament to those who were absent. As supervisors of eucharistic visitors, the new deacons may instead give them the sacrament to carry to the absent. If Prayer D is used (Canadian Prayer 6), the bishop names the new deacons in the remembrance clauses.

If only one deacon is ordained, the new deacon functions as deacon of the mass starting with the preparation of the table. If two or more deacons are ordained, they share functions as the bishop directs. (See the appendix for detailed functions of deacons in the Ordination of Deacons.)

## CELEBRATION OF A NEW MINISTRY

Much criticized for its emphasis on clerical status and for its use of ordination symbolism, this rite is used mainly to institute priests as rectors of parishes. On occasion, it may also be used to install a deacon into a congregation, chaplaincy, or other ministry. "The new minister, if a deacon, should read the Gospel, prepare the elements at the Offertory, assist the celebrant at the Altar, and dismiss the congregation" (BCP 558). The assembly gives symbols appropriate for the diaconate, such as a book of the gospels, a towel and basin (perhaps with washing of feet), and an oil stock. Elsewhere, "deacons assist according to their order" (BCP 558).

The supplemental rite in *Enriching Our Worship 4* (Church Publishing, 2007), titled "The Renewal of Ministry with the Welcoming of a New Rector or Other Pastor," is designed only for priests. The rubrics discourage its use for other ministers, and it should not be blended with the prayer book liturgy. Since the rite takes place within the Eucharist, deacons function as usual.

## THE DEDICATION AND CONSECRATION OF A CHURCH

Deacons attend the bishop as usual and function according to order. For the prayers of the people, "some other form may be composed for the occasion, having due regard for the distinctive nature of the community, and with commemoration of benefactors, donors, artists, artisans, and others" (BCP 576).

## OTHER LITURGIES WITH A BISHOP

### Consecration of Chrism Apart from Baptism (BOS 330–332; BAS 616–622)

The rite takes place after the postcommunion prayer in the Eucharist. "If desired, the vessel of oil may be brought forward in the offertory procession, received by a deacon or other minister, and then placed on a convenient side table until needed" (BOS 330). After the postcommunion prayer, a deacon brings the vessel to the bishop and, according to an old custom, may say aloud: "The oil for the holy chrism." (In Canada, the blessing of oils occurs near the end of the eucharistic prayer.)

In many dioceses, the rite takes place at a Chrism Mass, during the day on Maundy Thursday or earlier in Holy Week. The bishop blesses chrism for the whole diocese during the coming year, or for baptisms throughout the diocese at the Easter Vigil. If the bishop also blesses oil of the sick, a deacon brings the vessel to the bishop and may say aloud: "The oil of the sick."

## REAFFIRMATION OF ORDINATION VOWS (BOS 333–336)

The rite is used at a gathering of priests (and deacons) with their bishop. It is appropriate in the Eucharist at a conference or retreat or at the college of presbyters. Sometimes the rite takes place at the Chrism Mass on Maundy Thursday or earlier in Holy Week, although its use at that liturgy tends to cast a shadow on the blessing of oils. In some dioceses, the bishop and deacons reaffirm their vows at a separate meeting of the community of deacons. This practice avoids confusing deacons with priests.

Two deacons attend the bishop, and the deacon of the mass serves as usual by proclaiming the gospel and ministering at the altar (see chapter 3). The intercessions may be omitted, or they may take place after the peace.

The bishop may also use the rite to receive a priest (but not a deacon) from another communion, or to restore a priest or deacon to the ordained ministry. The restored deacon, "properly vested, prepares the bread and wine at the Offertory" (BOS 336).

## A SERVICE FOR THE ENDING OF A PASTORAL RELATIONSHIP AND LEAVE-TAKING FROM A CONGREGATION (BOS 339–346)

The rite is normally used when a priest-in-charge leaves a congregation. Two deacons normally attend the bishop, if present, and the deacon of the mass functions as usual in the Eucharist.

Otherwise, a single deacon functions as usual. If the bishop is absent, a deacon may act as the bishop's deputy.

## RECOGNITION AND INVESTITURE OF A DIOCESAN BISHOP (BOS 349–355)

In its fullest use, the rite provides for the recognition, investiture, and seating (usually in the cathedral) of a diocesan bishop. "Representative presbyters, deacons, and lay persons are assigned appropriate duties in the service" (BOS 348). From the start, the knocking on the door, the new bishop is "attended by two deacons" (BOS 349). Deacons prepare the table and gifts, and a deacon dismisses the people.

## WELCOMING AND SEATING OF A BISHOP IN THE CATHEDRAL (BOS 357–359)

Used separately, the rite completes the recognition and investiture of a diocesan bishop. Again, the new bishop, from the knocking on the door, is "attended by two deacons" (BOS 357). A deacon dismisses the people.

## SETTING APART FOR A SPECIAL VOCATION (BOS 360–364)

Religious orders have their own rites for the novitiate, temporary or annual vows, and life profession. This rite is used for individual persons taking vows directly under the diocesan bishop. Two deacons normally attend the bishop. If the rite occurs within the Eucharist, the deacon of the mass functions as usual.

# APPENDIX

This appendix contains lists of what deacons do in the Eucharist, baptism, liturgies of Holy Week, bishop's visitation, and ordinations. It also has some drawings to help deacons figure out when bishops should have "Hats Off!" and "Sticks On!"

## EUCHARIST
*(normal congregational setting)*

GETTING READY
Vest in alb and stole over left shoulder (and sometimes
    dalmatic).
Remove watches and jewelry, wash hands.
Oversee preparation of others.
Pray (with others).

GATHERING
Enter ahead of (if carrying gospel book) or at right side of
    presider.

Carry gospel book slightly elevated and place it, flat and face
     down, on center of altar.
[Assist with putting on incense, by holding boat.]
Sit at right of presider or in other nearby place.

GOSPEL
Bow before presider and ask for blessing.
Take book from altar and follow procession.
Announce gospel (perhaps chanted), right thumb marking
     cross on book, forehead, lips, heart.
[Cense book—center, left, right.]
Proclaim gospel—slowly and clearly.
End "The gospel of the Lord" (perhaps chanted) and kiss
     opening word.
Leading procession, take book back to altar.

PRAYERS OF THE PEOPLE
Presider or deacon introduces prayers.
Go to place (ambo or midst of congregation).
Sing or say biddings (with others).
Presider prays collect, and deacon returns to seat.
[Lead confession of sin, here or at beginning.]
Lead people in exchanging peace.

PREPARATION OF THE TABLE
Prepare table: remove gospel book, spread corporal, place
     plate and cup on right side.
Receive gifts: take bread and wine; place them on right side.
Prepare gifts: place bread on plate, pour wine and a little
     water in cup (and flagons).

Place gifts: place plate and cup, and perhaps flagons, on
    corporal.
[Assist with putting on incense, by holding boat.]
[Cense presider and people, perhaps walking among them.]

EUCHARISTIC PRAYER
Stand to right of presider, two or three steps behind, if
    possible.
At doxology, lift cup (while presider lifts bread).
At fraction, fill other cups from flagons and place on altar.
At invitation to communion, lift cup (as presider lifts bread).

COMMUNION
Assist in giving wine or bread, or oversee communion.
Clear altar of vessels and corporal.
At altar or elsewhere (here or after dismissal), consume
    leftover bread and wine and clean cups and flagons with
    water (with others), or oversee ablutions.
Distribute communion kits to eucharistic visitors.
Return to seat for postcommunion prayer (and
    announcements).

DISMISSAL
[In Lent, before solemn prayer over people, sing or say, "Bow
    down before the Lord."]
Sing or say dismissal, preferably right after blessing, or at
    least in front of people.
[In Easter, sing or say dismissal with "alleluia, alleluia."]
Leave ahead of or at right side of presider (leave gospel book
    behind).

## BAPTISM

Lead procession to font, bearing paschal candle.

May lead prayers for candidates.

May baptize, by immersion or pouring.

Light candles from paschal candle and give to newly
    baptized (or parents or godparents).

Bearing paschal candle, lead procession back to chancel for
    chrismation and reception.

Help give first communion to newly baptized.

## SEASONAL LITURGIES

PALM SUNDAY

Proclaim palm gospel as on Sunday or feast.

Start palm procession with "Let us go forth in peace."

Join in singing or reading passion gospel.

MAUNDY THURSDAY

Take part in washing feet.

Help presider take sacrament to place of reservation.

Take part in stripping altar.

No dismissal.

GOOD FRIDAY

Enter as usual and kneel or lie prostrate for a time before
    altar.

Join in singing or reading passion gospel.

Sing or say biddings in Solemn Collects.

Bring wooden cross into church for veneration, singing or
    saying three times, "Behold the wood of the cross, on
    which hung the Savior of the world."

Prepare altar and bring sacrament from place of reservation.

No dismissal.


EASTER VIGIL

Carry paschal candle into church, stopping three times and
    singing "The Light of Christ."

Place candle in holder.

Assist with putting on incense, holding boat.

Bow before presider and ask for blessing.

Cense candle, walking around it counterclockwise.

Sing Exsultet near candle (after salutation, extend hands for
    rest of chant).

Assist in baptism as usual.

Assist in Eucharist as usual.

Sing dismissal with "alleluia, alleluia" (Hymnal S 175), here
    and during the great fifty days.

## BISHOP'S VISITATION

### ENTRANCE

Carrying gospel book, walk ahead of bishop and place book
  on altar.
Take mitre from bishop (and staff, if no other attendant).
Bow to altar, with bishop.
[Assist with incense.]
Go to chair or remain near bishop.
Prop staff in a convenient place (or give to other attendant).
Here and elsewhere, may hold book for bishop.

### READINGS

Give mitre to bishop.
Sit in chair provided.
If hymn is sung before gospel, give book/music to bishop.

### GOSPEL

[Help prepare incense by holding boat.]
Bow deeply and ask for blessing.
Take mitre and lay aside.
Give staff to bishop.
Take gospel book from altar and join procession.
[Cense book and] say or sing gospel.
Return [and give book to bishop to kiss].
Put book back on altar or elsewhere.
Take staff from bishop.
Sit during sermon.

BAPTISM AND CONFIRMATION
For presentation, give mitre to bishop, stand at right.
Take mitre for prayers.

BAPTISM
Attend bishop in procession to font [may carry paschal
    candle].
At font, take mitre and hold during blessing of water.
[May hold vessel of oil before bishop for blessing of chrism.]
During water baptisms, give mitre to bishop.
Attend bishop on return to chair.
Take mitre and hold for prayer "Heavenly Father."
For chrismation, give mitre to bishop. May hold book for
    bishop.

CONFIRMATION, RECEPTION, REAFFIRMATION
Take mitre and hold or put aside for prayer before
    confirmation.
Hold book for bishop for prayer and confirmations.
After confirmations, etc., and following prayer, give mitre to
    bishop.

LITURGY OF THE TABLE
Prepare table, receive and prepare gifts, place on table.
Take mitre and put aside [and assist in censing].
[Remove bishop's skullcap before eucharistic prayer.]
During eucharistic prayer, stand at bishop's right, two steps
    back (if possible).
At end of prayer, raise cup when bishop raises bread.
Fill additional cup(s) at fraction.

Raise cup at invitation to communion.
Oversee communion and give wine or bread.
[Give bishop skullcap.]
Clear altar and consume remaining sacrament.

DISMISSAL
[Announcements.]
Give mitre and staff to bishop for blessing.
Sing or say dismissal (in Easter with "alleluia, alleluia"),
    preferably right after blessing, or at least in front of
    people.
Reverence altar with bishop and walk out ahead of bishop.

## ORDINATION OF A BISHOP

DEACON OF THE MASS
Enter ahead of Presiding Bishop (and concelebrants),
    carrying gospel book.
Proclaim liturgical gospel.
Prepare table, receive and prepare bread and wine, place on
    table.
Cense bishops (and people).
Remove new bishop's skullcap (if any) before eucharistic
    prayer.
During eucharistic prayer, attend near new bishop's right and
    raise cup during doxology.
At fraction, lead other deacons in preparing more plates and
    cups.
Raise cup at invitation to communion.

Assist in administering communion.

Lead other deacons in ablutions.

Sing or say dismissal (in Easter with "alleluia, alleluia"), right after blessing.


Two Deacons Attending the Presiding Bishop

In procession, walk a step behind Presiding Bishop.

Except during eucharistic prayer until end of communion, remain at PB's side.

Right deacon: Handle mitre and primatial staff.

Left deacon: Hold book containing order of service, open for PB to use.


Two Deacons Attending the New Bishop

Until end of ordination prayer, remain apart from bishop-elect.

During hymn to Holy Spirit, may hold book of gospels (open and face down) over head of kneeling bishop-elect.

Assist with vesting and giving symbols to new bishop.

Except during eucharistic prayer until end of communion, remain at new bishop's side.

Right deacon: hold mitre.

Left deacon: hold crozier.

In final procession, walk a step behind new bishop.

Other deacons may assist in preparing gifts, filling more cups, giving communion, and performing ablutions, as needed.

☩

## ORDINATION OF A PRIEST

DEACON OF THE MASS

Enter ahead of bishop (and concelebrants), carrying gospel book.

Proclaim liturgical gospel.

Assist in ordination with book, Bible, paten and chalice, or as needed.

Prepare table, receive and prepare bread and wine, and place on table.

Cense bishop (and people).

Remove bishop's skullcap (if any) before eucharistic prayer.

During eucharistic prayer, attend near bishop's right and raise cup during doxology.

At fraction, lead other deacons in preparing more plates and cups.

Raise cup at invitation to communion.

Assist in administering communion.

Lead other deacons in ablutions.

Sing or say dismissal (in Easter with "alleluia, alleluia"), right after blessing.


TWO DEACONS ATTENDING THE BISHOP

In procession, walk a step behind bishop.

Except during eucharistic prayer until end of communion, remain at bishop's side.

Right deacon: Hold mitre and pastoral staff.

Left deacon: Hold book containing order of service, open for
    bishop to use.

In final procession, walk a step behind bishop.

Other deacons may assist in preparing gifts, filling more
    cups, giving communion, and performing ablutions, as
    needed.

## ORDINATION OF DEACONS

DEACON OF THE MASS

Enter ahead of bishop (and concelebrants), carrying gospel
    book.

Proclaim liturgical gospel.

Assist in ordination with book, Bible, gospel book, vesting,
    or as needed.

*After ordination prayer, a new deacon takes over as deacon of
    the mass.*

Prepare table, receive and prepare bread and wine, and place
    on table.

Cense bishop (and people).

Remove bishop's skullcap (if any) before eucharistic prayer.

During eucharistic prayer, attend near bishop's right and
    raise cup during doxology.

At fraction, lead other deacons in preparing more plates and
    cups.

Raise cup at invitation to communion.

Assist in administering communion.

Lead other deacons in ablutions.

[One or all new deacons] sing or say dismissal (in Easter with "alleluia, alleluia"), right after blessing.

## TWO DEACONS ATTENDING THE BISHOP
In procession, walk a step behind bishop.

Except during eucharistic prayer until end of communion, remain at bishop's side.

Right deacon: Hold mitre and pastoral staff.

Left deacon: Hold book containing order of service, open for bishop to use.

*After peace, two new deacons take over this role.*

In final procession, walk a step behind bishop.

## OTHER DEACONS
Other deacons may assist in preparing gifts, filling more cups, giving communion, and performing ablutions, as needed.

*Cartoon by Priscilla Maumus*

# ENDNOTES

1. Galley, who died in 1993, was my mentor in liturgy and wrote forewords for the early editions of this book.
2. Although Roman Catholic deacons stand during the eucharistic prayer, they kneel *de more* (normally or as a rule) during the epiclesis and words of institution (*Institutio Generalis Missalis Romani,* 179).
3. The practice of joining hands palm to palm comes from Germanic feudalism. It is part of the ceremony of investiture in office and of submission to an overlord, in which one places the joined hands between the palms of the overlord.
4. *Biblioteca Vaticana,* MS 9820. The illustration is reproduced in Thomas Forrest Kelly, *The Exultet in Southern Italy* (New York: Oxford University Press, 1996), front jacket.
5. See the liturgies sometimes shown at www.ktotv.com.
6. Paul V. Marshall, *The Bishop Is Coming! A Practical Guide for Bishops and Congregations* (New York: Church Publishing, 2007), 33.
7. In some cultures, such as the Navajo, it is considered bad luck to go counterclockwise, and the presider must go the other way.
8. In the Ambrosian and Mozarabic rites and some eastern liturgies, the readers of lessons before the gospel also receive a blessing from the presider.

9. Not every bishop may wish to kiss the book. Marshall recommends the ceremony in *The Bishop Is Coming!*, 33, 57.

10. This section on the prayers of the people appears in expanded form in Ormonde Plater, *Intercession: A Theological and Practical Guide* (Cambridge, Mass.: Cowley Publications, 1995), chap. 4.

11. Howard Galley declined to include this prayer in *The Ceremonies of the Eucharist* (Cambridge, Mass.: Cowley Publications, 1989). He objected to the parallel metaphor, which suggests that the water will become divine and the wine human, or vice versa, since consecrated wine, as the blood of Christ, contains both the divine and the human natures. This interpretation seems forced. It is the mixed wine that becomes the two natures. Actually, both the bread and the wine (with or without water) will possess the fullness of Christ's divinity and humanity.

12. Although Howard Galley suggests that deacons use this prayer after filling the additional cups (*Ceremonies of the Eucharist*, 162), at that point they often are busy with preparations. The text, partly from Proverbs 9:1–2, was proposed as an offertory prayer in the first draft of the 1970 *Missale Romanum*; Galley rescued the prayer for Anglican use.

13. Howard E. Galley, *The Prayer Book Office* (New York: Seabury Press, 1980), 107.

14. Galley, *Prayer Book Office*, 360.

15. For a full treatment of the Candlemas procession, see Leonel L. Mitchell, *Pastoral and Occasional Liturgies: A Ceremonial Guide* (Cambridge, Mass.: Cowley Publications, 1998), 38–40.

16. For the ceremonies of the paschal cycle, see Leonel L. Mitchell, *Lent, Holy Week, Easter, and the Great Fifty Days: A Ceremonial Guide* (Cambridge, Mass.: Cowley Publications, 1996).

17. The music for the passion gospel, in downloadable form, may be found in *The Passion Gospels*, edited by Ormonde Plater (New York: Church Publishing Corporation, 2007).

18. This hymn has an origin connected with a famous woman deacon in the sixth century. Venantius Fortunatus wrote the poem *Pange lingua gloriosa* in honor of a fragment of the true cross given to his friend Radegund of Poitiers, deacon, queen, and monastic founder, c. 569.

19. Galley, *Prayer Book Office,* 109–110.

20. The word "prerogative" appears in only two places in the prayer book. The other concerns bishops: "It is the bishop's prerogative, when present, to be the principal celebrant at the Lord's Table, and to preach the Gospel" (BCP 322, 354; see BAS 183).

21. Kelly, *The Exultet in Southern Italy.*

22. Marshall, *The Bishop Is Coming!,* 33.

23. For the Ordination of a Priest, a rubric states that after the presentation of a Bible, "other instruments or symbols of office may be given" (BCP 553). The lack of a similar rubric for new deacons may be an oversight. In the Church of England the bishop may (present a towel and basin and) wash the feet of the new deacons. See "The Ordination of Deacons," *Common Worship: Ordination Services Study Edition* (London: Church House Publishing, 2007), and http://www.cofe.anglican.org/worship/liturgy/commonworship/texts/ordinal/deacons.html.

Printed in the USA
CPSIA information can be obtained
at www.ICGtesting.com
JSHW082213140824
68134JS00014B/599

9 780898 696349